Numbers and the number system 3

Teacher's handbook

GENERAL EDITORS   Sandy Cowling

Jane Crowden

Andrew King

Jeanette Mumford

CAMBRIDGE
UNIVERSITY PRESS

PUBLISHED BY THE PRESS SYNDICATE OF THE UNIVERSITY OF CAMBRIDGE
The Pitt Building, Trumpington Street, Cambridge, United Kingdom

CAMBRIDGE UNIVERSITY PRESS
The Edinburgh Building, Cambridge CB2 2RU, UK   http://www.cup.cam.ac.uk
40 West 20th Street, New York, NY 10011-4211, USA   http://www.cup.org
10 Stamford Road, Oakleigh, Melbourne 3166, Australia
Ruiz de Alarcón 13, 28014 Madrid, Spain

First published 2000

Printed in the United Kingdom at the University Press, Cambridge

Typefaces Frutiger, Swift   *System* QuarkXPress® 4.03

A catalogue record for this book is available from the British Library

ISBN 0 521 78455 7 paperback

General editors for Cambridge Mathematics Direct
Sandy Cowling, Jane Crowden, Andrew King, Jeanette Mumford

Writing team for *Numbers and the number system 3*
Mark Adams, Lynn Huggins-Cooper, Jeanette Mumford, Andrew King, Marian Reynolds

The writers and publishers would like to thank the many schools and individuals who trialled lessons for Cambridge Mathematics Direct.

Abbreviations and symbols

In the Teacher's handbook and textbook:

IP	Interactive picture	IP 4
TB	Textbook	6–7
CM	Copymaster	CM 21

A   is practice work
B   develops ideas
C   is extension work
★   if needed, helps with work in A

In the textbook:
A red margin indicates that activities are teacher-led.
A green margin indicates that activities are independent.

In the Teacher's handbook:
Italic text has been used for questions for the teacher to ask.
T-led = Teacher-led activity
Ind = Independent activity

Contents

Introduction to Fractions   **80**

Matching to the NNS Framework objectives

This grid matches Cambridge Mathematics Direct lesson objectives to the teaching programme from the National Numeracy Strategy *Framework for teaching mathematics*, to help you in creating your own organisation of the lessons. See page 10 for ways you can do this.

Framework objectives	Lessons
Counting and properties of numbers	

Count larger collections by grouping them
• count reliably a set of objects and tally, grouping in 10s, then other numbers	N 1.1

Describe and extend number sequences:
count on or back in 1s, 10s or 100s, starting from any 2- or 3-digit number
• count on or back in 1s or 10s, crossing 100	N 1.2
• count on or back in 1s, 10s and 100s, to at least 1000	N 1.3

Describe and extend number sequences:
count on or back in 2s starting from any 2-digit number; recognise odd and even numbers
• count on from 0 or 1 in steps of 2 to about 50	N 2.1, 2.2
• count on or back in steps of 2 starting from any 2-digit number	N 2.1
• recognise odd and even numbers to at least 100	N 2.1, 2.2, 2.3, 4.1

Describe and extend number sequences:
count on in steps of 3, 4 or 5 from any small number to at least 50, then back again
• count on in steps of 2, 3, 4. 5, 10 or 100 from any small number then back again	N 1.2, 3.1, 4.5
• describe and continue sequences formed in 5 x 5 and 6 x 6 grids	N 3.2
• create sequences with a given constraint	N 3.2

Recognise 2- and 3-digit multiples of 2, 5 or 10, and 3-digit multiples of 50 and 100
• count in 50s to 1000	N 3.4
• recognise 2- and 3-digit multiples of 2, 5 and 10: multiples of 10 are also multiples of 5	N 3.3, 4.4, 4.5
• recognise 3-digit multiples of 50 and 100: multiples of 100 are also multiples of 50	N 3.4

Place value and ordering	

Read and write numbers to at least 1000 in figures and words
• read and write whole numbers to at least 500 in figures and words	PV 1.1
• read and write whole numbers to at least 1000 in figures and words	PV 2.1, 3.1

Know what each digit in a 3-digit number represents and
partition 3-digit numbers into hundreds, tens and ones (HTU)
• know what each digit represents	PV 1.1, 3.1
• partition as, say 749 = 700 + 40 + 9	PV 1.1, 3.1
• recognise 0 as a place holder in 3-digit numbers	PV 2.1

Read and begin to write the vocabulary of comparing and ordering
numbers, including ordinal numbers to at least 100;
compare 2 given 3-digit numbers and give a number which lies between them
• compare and order a set of familiar numbers	PV 1.3
• use, read and write ordinal numbers and abbreviations	PV 1.3
• compare 2 familiar numbers and find numbers between them	PV 2.3
• compare and order a set of 3-digit numbers and find numbers between	PV 3.1, 3.2, 3.3

Say the number that is 1, 10 or 100 more or less than any given 2- or 3- digit number
• investigate number patterns by successively adding or subtracting 1, 10 or 100 to and from numbers up to 500	PV 1.2
• investigate number patterns by successively adding or subtracting 1, 10 or 100 to and from numbers up to 500	PV 2.2

Order whole numbers to at least 1000, and position them on a number line
• order a set of familiar numbers	PV 1.3
• order whole numbers to at least 1000, and position them on a number line	PV 3.1, 3.2, 3.3
• state a number lying between 2 numbers	PV 3.2

Estimating and rounding

Read and begin to write the vocabulary of estimation and approximation;

give a sensible estimate of up to about 100 objects

• make sensible estimates for numbers and collections to about 100	R 1.1
• estimate the position of a number on a number line	R 1.2
• explain how estimates are made and justify why they are reasonable	R 1.1, 1.2

Round any 2-digit number to the nearest 10 and any 3-digit number to the nearest 100

• round numbers less than 100 to the nearest 10	R 1.2, 1.3
• begin to approximate by rounding any 3-digit number to the nearest 100	R 1.3

Fractions

Recognise unit fractions and use them to find fractions of shapes and numbers to 20

• recognise and create the fractions $\frac{1}{2}$, $\frac{1}{3}$, $\frac{1}{4}$, $\frac{1}{5}$, $\frac{1}{10}$ using shapes	F 1.1, 1.5, 2.4, 3.5
• know that, say 10 tenths make 1 whole	F 1.1
• recognise what is not $\frac{1}{2}$, $\frac{1}{3}$, $\frac{1}{4}$, $\frac{1}{5}$, $\frac{1}{10}$	F 1.2
• identify $\frac{1}{2}$, $\frac{1}{3}$, $\frac{1}{4}$, $\frac{1}{5}$, $\frac{1}{10}$ of sets of objects to 20	F 1.3, 3.5
• find $\frac{1}{2}$ of all numbers to 30	F 1.3
• solve problems involving fractions	F 1.4, 1.5, 3.5

Begin to recognise simple fractions that are several parts of a whole

• recognise $\frac{3}{4}$	F 2.2
• recognise $\frac{2}{3}$	F 2.1, 2.2
• recognise tenths	F 2.3, 2.5
• know that, say $\frac{3}{10} + \frac{7}{10} = 1$	F 2.4
• find non-unit fractions of sets of objects to 20	F 2.5

Begin to recognise simple equivalent fractions

• recognise the equivalence of $\frac{1}{2}$ and $\frac{2}{4}$	F 2.2, 2.5
• recognise the equivalence of $\frac{5}{10}$ and $\frac{1}{2}$	F 2.3, 2.5
• know that, say $\frac{3}{5} + \frac{2}{5} = 5$ fifths and makes 1 whole	F 1.1, 2.5, 3.5

Compare familiar fractions

• position $\frac{1}{4}$, $\frac{1}{2}$, $\frac{3}{4}$ on a unit number line	F 3.1
• mark quarters, halves, three quarters on a number line to 10	F 3.2
• compare and order fractions involving halves and tenths	F 3.3
• investigate a general statement about ordering	F 3.5

Estimate a simple fraction

• make estimates of fractions of shapes and quantities in context	F 3.4

Reasoning about numbers or shapes

Solve mathematical problems or puzzles, recognise simple patterns and relationships, generalise and predict. Suggest extensions by asking 'What if...?'	N 2.3, 3.2, 4.1, 4.2, 4.3, 4.4, 4.5 PV 1.2, 2.2 F 1.4, 3.5
Investigate a general statement about familiar numbers or shapes by finding examples that match it	N 2.2, 4.4, 4.5 PV 2.4, F 1.4, 3.5
Explain methods and reasoning about numbers orally and, where appropriate, in writing	N 4.3, 4.4

Some learning objectives are covered in several lessons.

Lessons appear more than once in the grid if they cover several objectives.

About Cambridge Mathematics Direct

What is Cambridge Mathematics Direct?

Cambridge Mathematics Direct provides everything you need to plan, teach and assess your daily maths lesson in a simple, manageable way.

Cambridge Mathematics Direct is in line with the recommendations of the National Numeracy Strategy and places a strong emphasis on whole-class teaching, oral and mental work and direct communication with pupils. It directly reflects the philosophy and content of the *Framework for teaching mathematics*, providing comprehensive coverage of the learning objectives for each year.

Learning objectives have been grouped into three strands: Numbers and the number system; Calculations; and Measures, shape, space and handling data. Solving problems is included throughout. Each strand has been divided into mathematical **topics** consisting of **blocks of lessons**, that provide total coverage of the learning objectives for the year.

The following example shows how the strand Numbers and the number system is broken down. Each strand is broken down in a similar way.

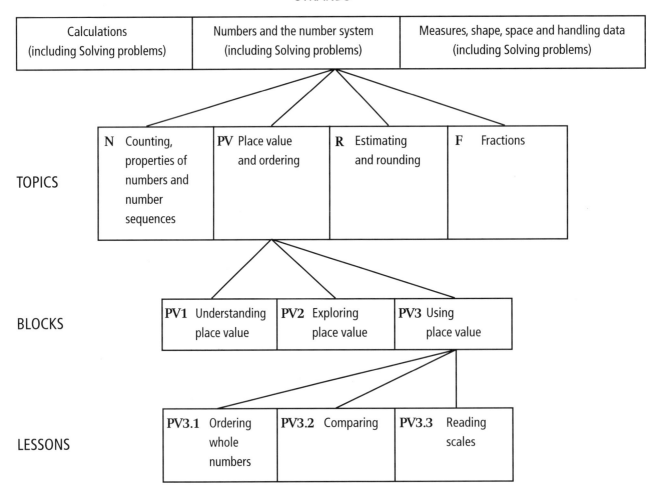

STRANDS

| Calculations (including Solving problems) | Numbers and the number system (including Solving problems) | Measures, shape, space and handling data (including Solving problems) |

TOPICS

N Counting, properties of numbers and number sequences

PV Place value and ordering

R Estimating and rounding

F Fractions

BLOCKS

PV1 Understanding place value

PV2 Exploring place value

PV3 Using place value

LESSONS

PV3.1 Ordering whole numbers

PV3.2 Comparing

PV3.3 Reading scales

The materials in Cambridge Mathematics Direct 3

Numbers and the number system	Calculations	Measures, shape, space and handling data
Teacher's handbook	Teacher's handbook	Teacher's handbook
Interactive pictures		Interactive pictures
Textbook	Textbook	Textbook
Copymasters	Copymasters	Copymasters

Teacher's handbooks

Each Cambridge Mathematics Direct teacher's handbook contains the following sections:

1 Planning with Cambridge Mathematics Direct

Ideas on how to organise your daily maths lessons using the lesson plans in Cambridge Mathematics Direct. There is also a blueprint on pages 12–13 that explains the features of the plans.

2 Matching to the NNS Framework for teaching mathematics objectives

Cambridge Mathematics Direct 3 covers all the learning objectives for Year 3 in the *Framework for teaching mathematics*. Concepts appear at least once in the material. The planning grid on pages 6–7 shows how lessons in *CMD Numbers and the number system 3* match to the *Framework*. Use it to find the learning objectives you are interested in.

3 Mental maths

Each lesson plan contains ideas for oral and mental maths, related to the objectives of the lesson. When there are particular skills you want to concentrate on, e.g. revising skills from earlier lessons or preparing for a future lesson, you can substitute different activities. The Oral work and mental calculation ideas bank on pages 14–16 will help with this.

Refer to this section when planning the oral and mental maths skills your class will focus on over a half-term. The activities in the *Numbers and the number system 3 Teacher's handbook* focus on skills relating to counting and place value.

4 Assessment

This section on pages 17–18 contains activities for assessing groups and individual children, together with written tasks for all key objectives

as part of your medium-term assessment.

Use the clear learning objectives in the planning grids to support you when you reflect on children's progress at the end of the year.

Each lesson plan provides opportunities for monitoring children's progress and identifying their misconceptions.

5 Lesson plans

Lessons follow the three-part structure recommended by the National Numeracy Strategy: oral and mental warm-up, followed by the main teaching activity (direct teaching and pupil activities) and then the plenary to review the concepts covered by the lesson.

The lesson plans are arranged in blocks within the relevant maths topic. Each topic begins with an introduction to the key concepts and vocabulary covered in the blocks.

Textbooks

The textbooks (TB) contain a variety of activities including word problems, games, open-ended activities, and pupil-generated ideas. There are whole-class activities, and group, paired and individual work.

Where there are activities in the textbook for a particular lesson they are grouped together under the lesson title. The 'key idea' for the lesson is given at the start of the activities. The work is differentiated as follows: support activities are shown by ★; activities for children of average ability are subdivided into easier activities (A) and harder activities (B); work to extend the most able pupils is denoted by C.

A red margin indicates that activities next to it are to be led by the teacher and those with a green margin are activities that children can do independently. Blue print shows children how to set their work out and red print tells them what resources they need.

Interactive pictures

Some of the lessons in *CMD Numbers and the number system 3* are based round interactive pictures. These A1-sized colour pictures prompt whole-class discussion and their content is related to the learning objectives for several lessons.

They are easy to use by clipping to an easel or fixing to a wall. Washable spirit pens may be used on their write-on, wipe-off surface.

Copymasters

The photocopiable sheets can be used in a variety of ways:

- Several of the pages provide general resources (e.g. 100 squares, number lines, place value cards).
- Some sheets are integral to a particular lesson and have been written to be used by the whole class, or by children doing core, support or extension work. You can differentiate the activity or change it slightly if you want children to repeat it, by altering the range of numbers before photocopying.
- Some pages are required for assessment activities.

Planning with Cambridge Mathematics Direct 3

The *Framework for teaching mathematics* and the National Curriculum specify which learning objectives are to be covered in Year 3. The order in which you teach these objectives will depend on your teaching plan for the year. You might be following the broad outline given by the half-termly plans in the *Framework*, your LEA's or school's scheme of work, or a plan that you have developed yourself. You can use Cambridge Mathematics Direct to follow all these plans. In addition, we suggest a specific order for teaching *Numbers and the numbers system 3* which provides a logical progression of concepts.

When planning, decide which areas of maths you want to teach and select the block or blocks of lessons that cover those objectives. The order

of lessons in a block has been chosen so that there is sensible development and progression of concepts. You can even pick out individual lessons if you prefer, as lessons are independent of each other. Activities in one lesson do not call upon items prepared in a previous lesson (although you will need to make sure that children have the understanding necessary to be able to tackle the new concepts you want to teach).

Using the lesson plans

The lesson plans in Cambridge Mathematics Direct teacher's handbooks have been provided as a starting point for the daily maths lesson but there is no need to follow them exactly. You could substitute activities that you have already found to be successful for those suggested.

There are several ways to use the lesson plans in Cambridge Mathematics Direct:

- You can dip in and out of the course choosing lessons where they fit in with the other resources you have in school.
- You can follow the half-termly plans suggested in the *Framework for teaching mathematics* and choose lessons from the planning grid that meet the objectives you are interested in.
- You can choose to teach complete blocks of lessons concentrating on one idea at the time. The following is a suggested order for teaching the lessons in Numbers and the number system 3 over the year.

Autumn term	
PV 1.1–1.3	Understanding place value
R 1.1	Estimating and rounding
N 1.1–1.3	Counting in ones, tens and hundreds
N 2.1–2.2	Twos
F 1.1–1.5	Simple fractions
Spring term	
PV 2.1–2.3	Exploring place value
N 3.1–3.4	Steps and multiples
N 2.3	Twos
F 2.1–2.5	Extending fractions
Summer term	
PV 3.1–3.3	Using place value
R 1.2–1.3	Estimating and rounding
N 4.1–4.5*	Reasoning about numbers
F 3.1–3.5	Comparing fractions

Lessons in the block marked * can be taught in any order.

Each lesson plan is arranged across a double-page spread. The blueprint on pages 12–13 explains what happens in each part of the lesson. It is not necessary to do everything in the lesson plan if you feel that some activities are not appropriate for the children in your class at that time. Questions for the teacher to ask are in italics.

Lesson structure

The structure of each lesson is in accordance with the recommendations of the National Numeracy Strategy. It provides a variety of approaches in the daily maths lesson and allows the concepts to be taught in the most suitable way.

The teaching model at the start of the lesson plan gives an overview of the structure of that particular lesson. It also shows where the teacher focus should be during the pupil activities. Lessons have been written so that groups of children receive similar amounts of teacher time over a block.

Each lesson contains fully differentiated pupil activities. Activities suitable for children working at the level specified for their year are called 'Core activities'. These are subdivided into easier activities (labelled A in the lesson plans and textbook) and harder activities (labelled B). The A activities practise and reinforce the concepts and skills taught during the direct teaching session. B tasks develop these ideas further.

Extension activities (labelled C) are included in every lesson. This work may be completed after B. Some more able children will be able to skip the A activities and start on B.

Some children need to revisit earlier work before they start something new. The support activities (denoted by ★) provide this extra experience. Once these children have completed the support activities they should be ready to move on to A.

The teaching model describes how children are to be grouped for the pupil activities. One of the activities will always be teacher-led. We expect that, during the pupil activities, the least able children will start with the Support activities and move onto the Core A activities, the average children will start with the Core A activities and move onto the Core B activities, and the most able children may start with the Core B activities and move on to the Extension activities. The teaching model shows both the first and second activities for each group.

Several different ways of organising this part of the lesson are included in Cambridge Mathematics Direct. The three ways used most often are:

- The class is split into three groups: Core, Least able and Most able and the teacher works with just one of the groups.
- The class is split into two groups: More able and Less able. The teacher works with one group or the other.
- The class is split into three groups at the start of the lesson: Least able working on Support, Core working on A and Most able working on B, and the teacher works with one group; later in the lesson, when the group has moved on to Core A, Core B, and Extension respectively, the teacher works with a different group.

Equipment needed

The equipment needed is specified in each lesson plan. The following are a few things that it would be useful to have at all times.

1. Packs of number cards
   - for a small group, enough 0–10 and 0–20 for each child
   - number word cards ('one', 'two'...)
2. Vocabulary and symbol cards
   $+, -, \times, \div, =$
   Add, subtract, take away, minus ...
3. Place value cards. You could use CM 62–64.
4. Playing cards
5. Dice and spinners (available from Tarquin 01379 384 218).
   Especially 1–6 and blank dice.
6. A variety of number lines. You could use CM 55–60 and IP 7.

How the daily lesson plans work

This is the main purpose of the lesson, which pupils can then focus on in the plenary.

These major objectives for the lesson relate directly to the *Framework for teaching mathematics*

This is a summary of how the lesson is organised. It shows where the main teacher input is required, how the children are grouped and what activities they may start and finish on.

These are warm-up activities which focus on rapid recall of number facts and mental strategies.

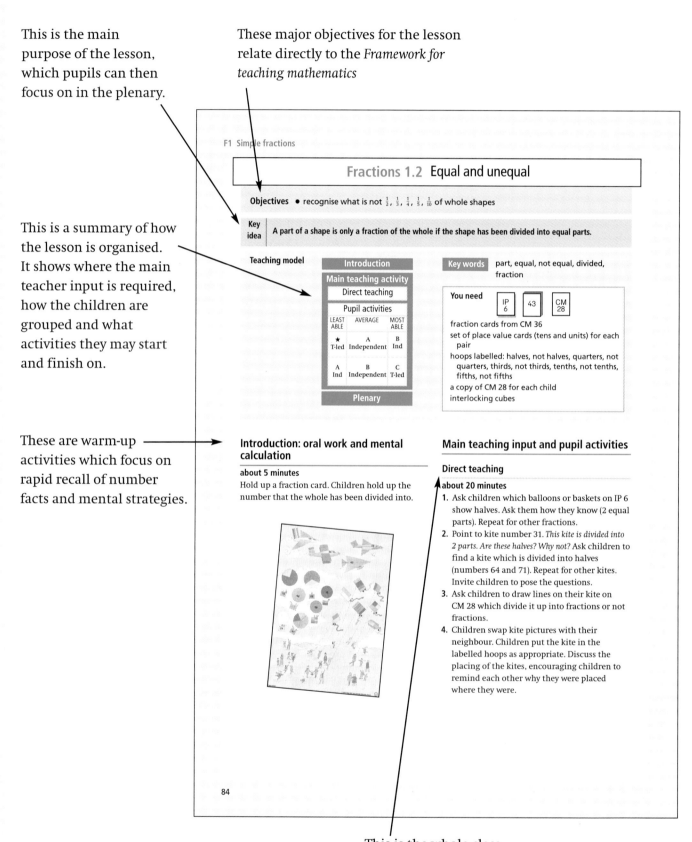

F1 Simple fractions

Fractions 1.2 Equal and unequal

Objectives • recognise what is not $\frac{1}{2}$, $\frac{1}{3}$, $\frac{1}{4}$, $\frac{1}{5}$, $\frac{1}{10}$ of whole shapes

Key idea | A part of a shape is only a fraction of the whole if the shape has been divided into equal parts.

Teaching model

| Introduction |
| Main teaching activity |
| Direct teaching |
| Pupil activities |

LEAST ABLE	AVERAGE	MOST ABLE
★ T-led	A Independent	B Ind
A Ind	B Independent	C T-led

| Plenary |

Key words part, equal, not equal, divided, fraction

You need IP 6 | 43 | CM 28
fraction cards from CM 36
set of place value cards (tens and units) for each pair
hoops labelled: halves, not halves, quarters, not quarters, thirds, not thirds, tenths, not tenths, fifths, not fifths
a copy of CM 28 for each child
interlocking cubes

Introduction: oral work and mental calculation

about 5 minutes
Hold up a fraction card. Children hold up the number that the whole has been divided into.

Main teaching input and pupil activities

Direct teaching

about 20 minutes
1. Ask children which balloons or baskets on IP 6 show halves. Ask them how they know (2 equal parts). Repeat for other fractions.
2. Point to kite number 31. *This kite is divided into 2 parts. Are these halves? Why not?* Ask children to find a kite which is divided into halves (numbers 64 and 71). Repeat for other kites. Invite children to pose the questions.
3. Ask children to draw lines on their kite on CM 28 which divide it up into fractions or not fractions.
4. Children swap kite pictures with their neighbour. Children put the kite in the labelled hoops as appropriate. Discuss the placing of the kites, encouraging children to remind each other why they were placed where they were.

84

This is the whole-class introduction, and includes questions you might ask pupils.

Work is aimed at the average ability pupils and divided into CORE A and CORE B in order to develop concepts and provide progression.

This indicates where the teacher focus should be.

Work to support the Least able pupils, which aims to enable them to move on to the CORE A activities.

Work to extend and challenge the Most able pupils. Sometimes these pupils will need to do CORE A and CORE B

This indicates where additional adult intervention would be most appropriate, if available.

These are ideas to discuss with the whole class, in relation to the work covered. It is an opportunity for you to pick up on misconceptions and focus on the key idea of the lesson.

Facsimile of textbook page to be used for these activities.

Facsimile of copymaster to be used for this activity.

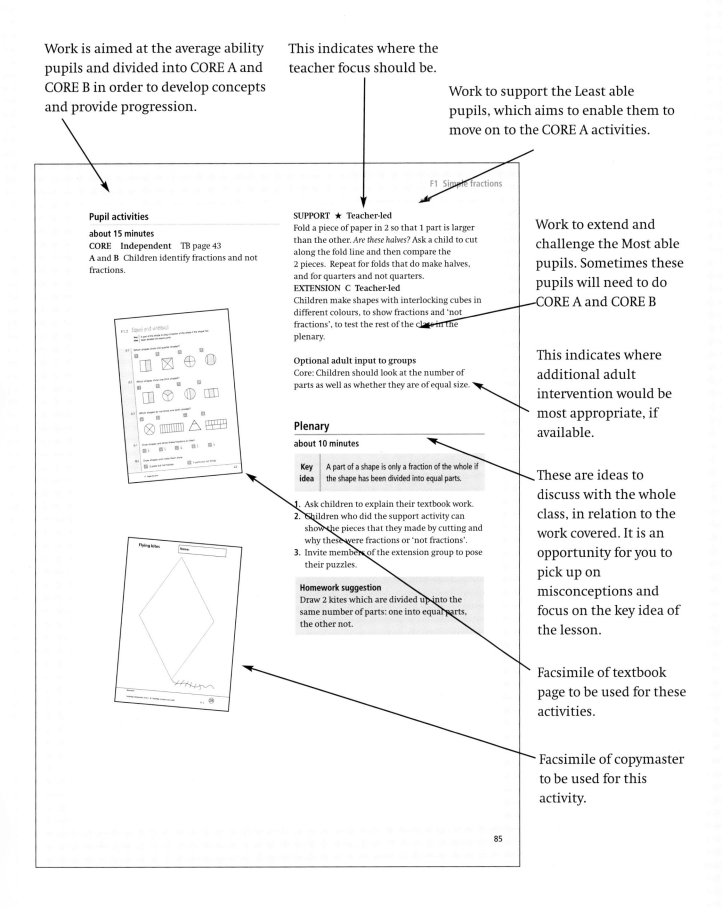

F1 Simple fractions

Pupil activities

about 15 minutes
CORE   Independent   TB page 43
A and B Children identify fractions and not fractions.

SUPPORT ★ Teacher-led
Fold a piece of paper in 2 so that 1 part is larger than the other. *Are these halves?* Ask a child to cut along the fold line and then compare the 2 pieces. Repeat for folds that do make halves, and for quarters and not quarters.
EXTENSION C Teacher-led
Children make shapes with interlocking cubes in different colours, to show fractions and 'not fractions', to test the rest of the class in the plenary.

Optional adult input to groups
Core: Children should look at the number of parts as well as whether they are of equal size.

Plenary

about 10 minutes

Key idea	A part of a shape is only a fraction of the whole if the shape has been divided into equal parts.

1. Ask children to explain their textbook work.
2. Children who did the support activity can show the pieces that they made by cutting and why these were fractions or 'not fractions'.
3. Invite members of the extension group to pose their puzzles.

Homework suggestion
Draw 2 kites which are divided up into the same number of parts: one into equal parts, the other not.

85

Oral work and mental calculation ideas bank

Use these short activities with the whole class or groups to practise and develop oral and mental maths skills. You can use them to supplement or replace the activities suggested in the oral introduction in the lesson plans or whenever you have a spare 5 minutes.

Counting, properties of numbers and number sequences

Steps of 1, 10 or 100

1. Count on and back from 0 in 1s, then 10s and then 100s. Vary the pace and direction of counting using a counting stick or number line as a guide, e.g. 1, 2, 3, 4, 5, 6, 7, 8, 9, 8, 7, ...; 10, 20, 30, 40, 50, 60, 70, 80, 70, 60, ...; 100, 200, 300, 400, 500, 400, 300, 200, ...

2. Count on and back in steps of 1, 10, 100 from 0 and then any 2- or 3-digit number:
   Start at 80. Count on in 1s to 110 and back to 80.
   Start at 80. Count on in 10s until you pass 200.
   Start at 80. Count on in 100s to 980.

3. Display a +1 card and explain that you are going to count up in 1s to 100 together. Point to IP 1 as you count.
   Show a −1 card and count back from 100 to 0.
   Repeat using +10, −10 cards.
   What makes counting in 10s easy?

4. Play 'Change':
   Use cards +1, −1, +10, −10, +100, −100.
   Begin counting around the class in 1s or 10s from any 2-digit number. After about 4 or 5 numbers, clap and point to a new operation to change the count. Continue counting on and back in multiples of 1, 10 and 100, between 0 and 500.

Steps of 3, 4, 5 or 10

5. Count in 3s, 4s and 5s to 100 from zero and back again.
   Start from 1 and other numbers.

6. Play 'To and fro':
   Make two large groups. Group 1 counts forwards. Group 2 counts backwards. Group 1 starts counting on in 10s from any single-digit number. When you clap your hands,

Group 2 counts backwards. The direction of the count changes every time you clap. Repeat the activity for steps of 2, 3, 4 or 5 to 30.

7. *Show me the next number in this pattern:*
   12, 10, 8, 6, ...; 110, 107, 104, 101, ...
   Ask children to describe the patterns and explain how they worked out what number would come next.

8. Make sticks of cubes, e.g. 3 red, 3 yellow, 3 red, 3 yellow, ... Use these to aid the quick recall of patterns of known multiples. Count multiples along the stick, e.g. 0, 3, 6, 9, ... Ask children to continue the pattern. Try multiples of other numbers, such as 5, 10, or 4 ...

9. Ask:
   What is the first multiple of 2/5/10 after 101?
   Where will we find all the multiples of 10/5?
   Tell me a multiple of 2/5/10 less than 140 / more than 180.
   What is the next multiple of 10/5 before/after 175?

10. Play 'Mechanical maze' on IP 3:
    Children can play in teams or as individuals. The maze consists of a series of chambers which contain a number of characters called Geotots. Tritot represents 3, Quadrotot 4 and Pentatot 5.
    The players/teams decide whether they are collecting 3s, 4s or 5s. They must all agree to collect the same number.
    Players colour in their balls in the bottom right hand corner of the IP and draw the route each ball takes through the maze to see how much they can score. When the player enters a chamber they count aloud in the number of steps they are collecting.
    Players may not double back on the route they have taken.
    A player's turn is over when they reach the 'Finish' in the dragon's mouth or find they have hemmed themselves into a corner.
    When the player leaves a chamber they add the score from that chamber to their running total. Players calculate their scores as they go but keep them secret until the end.
    Alternatively, use the maze for counting in

steps of 3, 4 or 5 with the whole class. Ask a child to draw a route through the maze first.

Odds, evens and counting in 2s

11. Count on and back in steps of 2 from 0 or 1 to 40/50.
12. Count to 40 and back in steps of 2 from 0 or 1 to 40/50.
13. Count on and back in steps of 2 from 2- and 3-digit numbers.
14. Hold up a number card. Children put up one hand if it is odd and two hands if it is even.
15. Play 'Neighbours':
    What are the next 3 odd/even numbers after 51/47/96, ...?
    What are the 3 odd/even numbers before 63/72/94/80, ...?
16. Play 'Fingers':
    Split the class into 2 teams: Evens and Odds. Choose 4 children. On a given signal, they each quickly hold up a number of fingers on one hand. Total the numbers shown. If the total is odd (even), Odds (Evens) win a point, e.g. if 2, 3, 4 and 5 are shown, the total is 14, so Evens win a point.

Place value and ordering

17. Play 'Next 10':
    Call out a 2-digit number and children hold up the next tens number.
    Play 'Last 10':
    Call out a 2-digit number and children hold up the tens number before it.
18. Choose a child to write a 2-digit number on the board. In unison, the class reads the number aloud and then says the number which is 10 less, then 10 more. Repeat for different children.
19. Ask children to use their place value cards (or similar).
    Give me a number between 10 and 20, 34 and 36, 50 and 100, 55 and 70, 120 and 140.
    Give me an odd/even number between 37 and 40, 60 and 170, 300 and 320.
    Give me a 3-digit number between 95 and 102, ...
20. Play 'Guess my number':
    Choose a child to write a 2-digit number on a piece of paper. Through 'yes'/'no' responses to

questions children establish the decade, whether the number is odd or even, and finally the units digit.
Extend to 3 digits.

21. Play 'Pass the paper':
    Ask one child in each group to write a 3-digit number on a scrap of paper, fold the paper and pass it to another child in the group. This child secretly unfolds the paper and whispers the number to a neighbour. The neighbour now writes the number on a large piece of paper looking to its originator to confirm the match.
    Repeat several times. Increase the number of children involved in passing on the whispered number.
22. Ask children to use their place value cards.
    Give me a number that:
    is an even/odd number greater/less than 50,
    is a 2-digit number with both digits even (odd),
    is a 2-digit number whose digits add up to 9/10/11,
    is a 2-digit number where the tens digit is double (half) the units digit.
    Locate all the possible answers to the last two questions on IP 1.
23. Play 'Zero in':
    My number is less than 600 and more than 200.
    It has 6 units.
    It has 0 in the tens place.
    What might my number be? (506, 406 or 306)
24. Play 'Place invaders':
    Write a 3-digit number on the board, e.g. 529. Give cards labelled 'U', 'T' and 'H' to 3 children. The child with 'U' begins, saying, '529, zapp the 9 leaves 520.' The child with 'T' says, '520, zapp the 20 leaves 500.' The child with 'H' says, '500, zapp the 500 leaves 0.' Repeat with other 3-digit numbers.
25. Play 'Elimination':
    Children stand up and each choose a 2-digit number.
    Sit down if:
    your number is odd (even);
    your number is a multiple of 10 (or 5);
    the tens digit is greater (or less) than the units digit;
    the sum of the digits is more than (or less than) 10;
    the units digit is 1 (or 2, 3, ... 9).
    Continue until all are eliminated but one, the winner.

Repeat several times, adjusting the conditions.
Extend to 3 digits.

26. Ask:
Something weighs more than 200 g and less than 300 g. What could it weigh?
John is taller than 1 m 3 cm and smaller than 1 m 40 cm. How tall could he be?

Fractions

27. Display a number line showing halves and quarters. Practise counting along and back in steps of a half and then a quarter.
Display the tenths number line. Call a number, e.g. $4\frac{2}{10}$, and ask children to write and show the number before or the number after.

28. Play 'Make one whole':
Call out a fraction, or hold up a fraction card e.g. $\frac{4}{10}$, and ask children to write and show the fraction needed to make it up to one whole ($\frac{4}{10}$). N.B. display number lines marked in tenths and halves/quarters to help children who need support.

29. Hold up a fraction card (CM 36). Children hold up the number that the whole has been divided into.

Number bonds

30. Play 'Make 10/20':
Call out a number. Children show the number to make it up to 10.
Call out 2 numbers. Children show the number needed to make their total up to 10/20.

31. *Work out 3 + 4, 6 + 1 + 5, 9 − 5 + 2, ...*
Work up to combining 4 numbers. Ensure that all children have made an answer before asking them to hold up their number cards.

32. Call out a number 0–20. *I'm thinking of a number. This is half of that number. Show me the number I'm thinking of.*

33. Hold up a number card to 20. Children, working in pairs, show the number that is half yours.

34. With children working in pairs, ask for doubles of numbers.

35. Call out tens numbers to 100. Children show half with place value cards.

The activities in this section can be used for medium-term assessment to review and record children's progress in relation to the key learning objectives you have covered during a half-term. Children's performance and any misconceptions that are revealed during the activities will help you with your next stage of medium-term planning.

The activities focus on the key objectives from the *Framework for teaching mathematics* (shown by a *). They have also been linked to the blocks of lessons in Cambridge Mathematics Direct that concentrate on these learning objectives. This enables you to choose an activity which assesses the work you have just been covering. Assessment activities have also been included for other important learning objectives.

Most of the activities are teacher-independent so that you can concentrate on how children approach the various tasks and assess their ability to explain their methods and reasoning.

Counting, properties of numbers and number sequences

N1 Count on or back in 10s or 100s from any 2- or 3-digit number.*
- Put children into groups of about four or five. Give each child a different coloured pen and a piece of paper. Ask them each to write their name and a 2-digit number at the top of the paper without anyone else seeing. They turn over the top of the paper so that no-one can see what they have written and pass the paper on to the next child. They look under the fold, add 10 to the number, write down the new number and fold the paper again. Continue passing the paper round. The use of the different coloured pens will enable you to see who can add 10.
  Repeat for adding and subtracting 100 to and from 3-digit numbers.
- Use CM 2 to assess how children add tens and hundreds.

N2 Count on or back in 2s; recognise odd and even numbers to at least 50.
- The activities on CM 45 check children's recognition of odd and even numbers.

N3 Count on or back in steps of 3, 4 or 5 from any small number to at least 50; recognise multiples of 2, 5 or 10.
- Children find the 'rule' on CM 46 and also make up their own sequence.
- Call out numbers and ask children to write down whether they are multiples of 2, 5 or 10.

N4 Explain methods and reasoning.*
- This may be assessed during the assessment of other concepts.

Place value

PV1 Read, write and order whole numbers to 500; know what each digit represents.*
- Change the numbers in words and figures on CM 15 to assess children's reading of numbers. Ask them to partition the numbers on the vests into hundreds, tens and units and then to order the numbers. Change the amounts of money at the bottom of the page.

PV2 Say the number that is 1, 10 or 100 more or less than any 2- or 3-digit number
- Use CM 47 to check that children understand which digits change and which digits stay the same when they add or subtract 10 or 100.

PV2 Know what each digit in a number represents; order whole numbers to 1000.*
- Give children a set of digit cards each. Ask them to pick 3 cards at random. They use these to make 3-digit numbers, partitioning them into hundreds, tens and units to check that they understand that the value of each digit is related to its position in a number. Ask children to order the numbers that they produce.

PV3 Order whole numbers to 1000; know what each digit represents.*

- Change the numbers on CM 22 to give children another opportunity to order numbers and find 'numbers between' selected numbers. Ask children to partition the numbers for the containers at the top of the page.

Estimating and rounding

R1 Give a sensible estimate; round any 2-digit number to the nearest 10 and any 3-digit number to the nearest 100.

- Use CM 48 to check children's rounding and estimating skills. Change the numbers to test again.

Fractions

F1 Recognise unit fractions such as $\frac{1}{2}$, $\frac{1}{3}$, $\frac{1}{4}$, $\frac{1}{5}$, $\frac{1}{10}$, and use them to find fractions of shapes and numbers.*

- Ask children to make shapes out of 30 cubes that are $\frac{1}{2}$ blue and $\frac{1}{10}$ red.
- CM 49 requires children to be able to find unit fractions of shapes and sets.

F2 Begin to recognise fractions that are several parts of a whole.

- Children identify fractions on CM 50.

F2 Begin to recognise equivalence of simple fractions.

- Change the numbers on CM 37 to assess children's understanding of the equivalence of fractions.

F3 Compare similar fractions

- Children order fractions on CM 51.

LESSON
PLANS

Glossary

Key words and terms to be used with children
count, tally, how many?, sequence, predict, continue, rule, relationship, odd, even, greatest, least, multiple, pattern, total, add, subtract, equals, check, equation, operation, consecutive

tally   a system using marks, usually grouped in 5s, for keeping a simple written record of a count

relationship   describes the link between 2 or more numbers or items in a sequence, for example 1, 5, 9, 13, ... where the relationship between the numbers is that each number is 4 greater than the number before it

rule   this is the calculation that has to be carried out to make numbers in a sequence, for example 1, 5, 9, 13, ... where the rule is that 4 is added each time

sequence   a set of numbers built up by using a given or agreed rule, for example 1, 5, 9, 13, ... where the rule is that 4 is added each time

multiple   if you start at 0 and count on in steps of a given size, then all the numbers in that sequence are multiples of that step, for example 0, 4, 8, 12, ... where the step is of 4 so the resulting numbers are all multiples of 4

general statement   tells you something about a set of numbers, such as 'an even number plus an even number makes an even number'

General overview of the topic

A good knowledge of counting patterns underpins arithmetic skills, e.g. knowing that counting in tens leaves the units digit unchanged makes adding 2-digit numbers much easier and also helps children to understand our place value system.

Knowing which counting patterns particular numbers belong to can also help when solving problems, e.g. knowing that 9 is an odd number means that you appreciate that 9 children cannot play a game in pairs without someone being left out.

It is very useful for children to learn to count on in given steps from any number, not only from 0. It is important that they are aware that the numbers generated by this are not always multiples of the step.

Numbers 1: Counting in ones, tens and hundreds
Children extend their counting skills to counting on in ones, tens or hundreds from any 2- or 3-digit number.

Numbers 2: Twos
This deals with identifying odd and even numbers and investigating how they behave in calculations.

Numbers 3: Steps and multiples
Children count on in steps of 2, 3, 4 and 5 from any number and look at the patterns that are formed.

Numbers 4: Reasoning about numbers
This encourages children to apply their knowledge of how numbers behave to different situations.

Links between blocks

Individual lessons from Numbers 4 may be taught after lessons in the other blocks, e.g. lesson N4.1 'Dice and dominoes' uses concepts covered in lessons in Numbers 2.

Before they start, children need to

- be familiar with numbers to 100
- know the value of digits in a 2-digit number
- have a working knowledge of odd and even numbers
- understand the term *sequence*

Concepts covered next year include

- 4-digit numbers
- alternating nature of odds and evens
- recognising multiples of 4s and 8s

Assessment points

- recognising odd and even numbers
- recognising multiples of 2, 5, 10, 50 and 100
- bridging the 100 boundary when counting in 10s or 100s

Chief misconceptions

- not realising that when you count in steps from any number, the numbers generated are not always multiples of the step
- believing that the numbers generated when counting in steps of 2 are always even regardless of whether the starting number is even or odd

Numbers 1.1 Counting collections

Objectives ● use, read and begin to write the vocabulary of counting
● count collections and tally by grouping in tens, then other numbers

Key idea	We can make counting easier by grouping. One way of counting using grouping is keeping a tally.

Teaching model

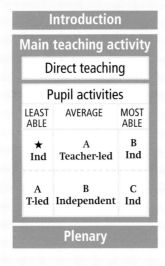

Key words   Count, tally, how many?

You need

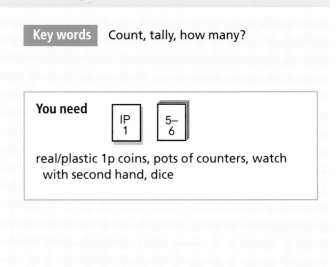

real/plastic 1p coins, pots of counters, watch with second hand, dice

Introduction: oral work and mental calculation

about 5 minutes

Count up and back in 1s, 10s and then 5s using IP 1 where necessary.

Main teaching input and pupil activities

Direct teaching

about 15 minutes

1. Tip out 1p coins. *How can we find out how many there are? Do we have to count in ones?*
2. Ask for three volunteers to count them by putting them in piles of 10. Record the subtotals on the board. Talk about the groups of 10. Discuss what to do with the remainders, combining them if possible. *How can we work out the total?* (Adding the three subtotals, counting the piles in 10s.) Ask children to suggest other ways of grouping the counters to find the total. *So, when we have a large collection of objects to count, we can group them to make counting easier.*

3. *Now, we're going to count using a different sort of grouping. Ask for a volunteer to jump up and down on the spot for one minute at the front. Record the number of jumps, grouping the marks in 10s. Why might it help to group the marks this way? How can we find out how many jumps there were altogether? Do we have to count each mark? This is called tallying.*

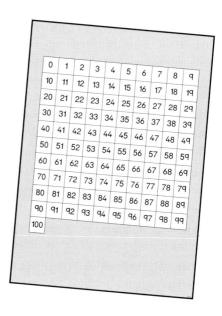

4. Explain that tallying is usually done in groups of five, the fifth stroke being the one that groups the marks from the top right to the bottom left as in a five bar gate. Knowing the 5 times table makes counting the tally marks much quicker. *Who can show us how to group the next set of jumps in this way?*

Pupil activities

about 20 minutes
CORE
A Teacher-led
In pairs, one child jumps for a minute while the other keeps a tally of the number of jumps. Children then change roles and a tally is kept of a new activity, e.g. the number of hops made.
B Independent TB pages 5–6
SUPPORT ★ Independent
In pairs, children count the counters in a pot by grouping in 10s and then in 5s to check.
EXTENSION C Independent   TB page 6
Here children are tallying as a running record of a number of outcomes. They can see from their tally when to stop.

Optional adult input to groups
Support: Check that children count in 10s and 5s rather than in ones.
Extension: Encourage children to keep an eye on the running totals.

Plenary

about 10 minutes

Key idea	We can make counting easier by grouping. One way of counting using grouping is keeping a tally.

1. Ask children who did the support activity to explain which form of tallying was easier to read.
2. *How did tallying help to count the totals in A? Did you need to count each mark?*
Talk about the different suggestions for grouping the jumps in B. Does the group size make any difference to the final total?

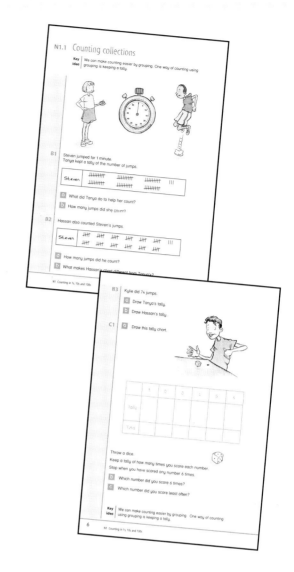

3. For children doing the extension activity, how useful were the tally marks for keeping a running total?
4. Discuss different ways we count groups in everyday life: money (coins weighed in banks), food multipacks, points in sports, ... *What would be the best way to count all the cubes in the tray, all the children in the school, ...?*

Homework suggestion
Children keep a tally of how many jumps, hops, claps, ... someone can do at home in a minute.

23

Numbers 1.2 Ones and tens beyond 100

Objective	● count on or back in 1s or 10s crossing 100 and from any 2- or 3-digit number

Key idea	We can count in ones and tens on and back from any 2-digit or 3-digit number.

Teaching model

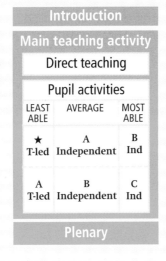

Key words   count

You need

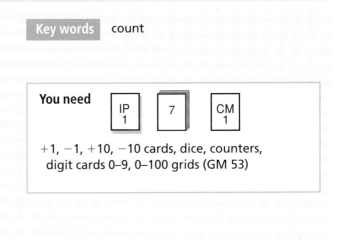

+1, −1, +10, −10 cards, dice, counters, digit cards 0–9, 0–100 grids (GM 53)

Introduction: oral work and mental calculation

about 5 minutes

Display the +1 card and explain that you are going to count up in 1s to 100 together.
Point to IP 1 as you count.
Show the −1 card and count back from 100 to 0.
Repeat using the remaining cards (+10, −10).
What makes counting in 10s easy?

Main teaching input and pupil activities

Direct teaching

about 15 minutes

1. Ask children to think of a number that they think no one else in the room will have thought of. Tell them to write it down together with the next number and the one before it. *Which number did you choose? What is the next number, what is the one before?* Children win a point for each number that no-one else has.
2. *Now, choose another number and this time count on 4 in 1s. Count back 4 in 1s. What were your numbers?* Has anyone scored 6 points?
3. *Count on from 153 to 159. How many did you count on?*

Count back from 287 to 281. How many did you count back?
Repeat for other numbers, posing 2-digit problems for less able children.

4. Ask children to think of a multiple of 10 and count 10 on and back from their chosen number. Remind children that counting on or back in 10s leaves units the same.
5. Now ask children to think of a number they think no-one else will think of and count on and back, in 10s.
6. *Now count on 40 in 10s. Count back 40 in 10s. What numbers did you have?*

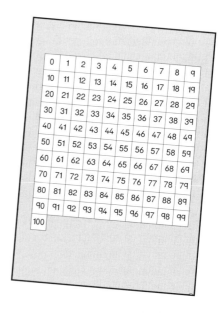

7. *Count on 30 in 10s from 24. Count on 30 in 10s from 645.*

8. Count on in 10s from 31 to 81. How many 10s did you count on?

 Count back in 10s from 93 to 53. How many 10s did you count back?

Pupil activities

about 20 minutes

CORE Independent

A CM 1

Play 'Getting to the shops'.

B TB page 7

SUPPORT ★ Teacher-led

Each small group needs a dice and 0–100 grid for support. Children start at 64, and throw a dice to find how many to count on, predicting where they will land before they count. First one to or past 100 wins. Repeat, playing from 0 with each dice throw a multiple of 10.

EXTENSION C Independent

Each pair needs a set of digit cards. Children start at 1000 and take turns to take the top digit card from a shuffled pack. Alternate digits for each player stand for units or multiples of 10, and are subtracted from the score. Children record their scores. First to 0 is the winner.

Optional adult input to groups

Core: Ensure that children are working out where they will land before counting squares to check.
Extension: Can children say which digits it is better to have as units and which as tens?

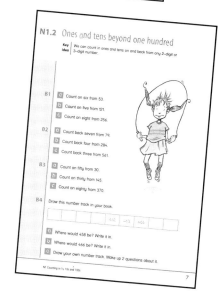

Plenary

about 10 minutes

Key idea	We can count in ones and tens on and back from any 2-digit or 3-digit number.

1. Ask children to talk about the records of the games they played. Which were really good rounds, where they moved quite quickly? Which were rounds where they made very little progress?

2. Ask ten children to stand in a line. Point to the seventh along. *If Robert is 348, who is 345?*

3. What do different children do to help them when they are counting in 1s or counting in 10s?

Homework suggestion
Starting with their street number count on 20, 50, 70 and 90 in 10s.

Numbers 1.3 Ones, tens and hundreds

Objectives
- count on or back in 1s, 10s or 100s, to at least 1000, from any small number
- describe and extend the sequences made
- predict start and finishing numbers for a given number of jumps

Key idea	We can count on and back in ones, tens and hundreds from any 2-digit or 3-digit number.

Teaching model

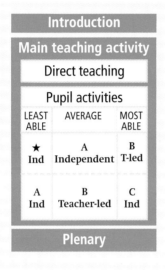

Key words count, sequence, predict, continue, relationship

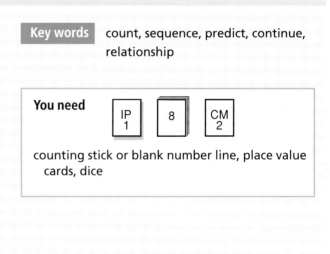

You need IP 1, 8, CM 2

counting stick or blank number line, place value cards, dice

Introduction: oral work and mental calculation

about 5 minutes

Explain that you are going to count on and back from zero in 1s, then 10s and then 100s. Vary the pace and direction of counting using a counting stick or number line as a guide, e.g.

1, 2, 3, 4, 5, 6, 7, 8, 9, 8, 7, ...
10, 20, 30, 40, 50, 60, 70, 80, 70, 60, ...
100, 200, 300, 400, 500, 400, 300, 200, ...

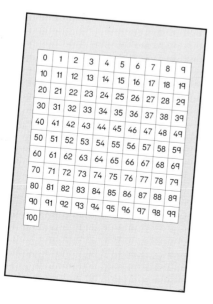

Main teaching input and pupil activities

Direct teaching

about 15 minutes

1. Count on in 10s round the class from 540. *Who will say 720?*
   Count back in 10s round the class from 540. *Who will say 360?*
2. Count on and then back 300 in 100s as a class from 600 ... from 630 ... from 680.
3. Count on in 100s from 530 to 830. *How many hundreds did you count?*
4. Remind children that a sequence is a set of numbers made or written in order according to a rule, e.g. adding 10 each time. Write this sequence on the board: 134, 234, 334, ... *Who can describe this sequence? What is the relationship between pairs of numbers? What would the next number be?* Repeat for other sequences: 79, 78, 77, ..., 546, 536, 526, ... Ask children to make up sequences for the class to work out.

Pupil activities

about 20 minutes
CORE

A Independent   CM 2

Playing in pairs, children take it in turns to choose one place value card from each set and roll a dice. They count on in 1s, 10s and 100s as appropriate from the number on each of the cards. Players check one another's counting and record their cards, dice throw and final numbers only.

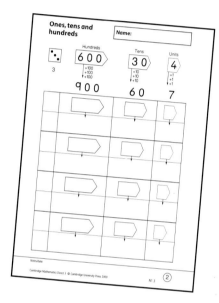

B Teacher-led   TB page 8

Children complete sequences and then make up their own.

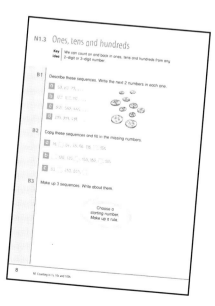

SUPPORT ★ Independent CM 2

Make CM 2 easier by providing a dice labelled 1, 1, 2, 2, 3, 3. Give children an extra set of place value cards to help them model the numbers.

EXTENSION C Independent CM 2

Allow players to play CM 2 counting *back* from the numbers on the cards. What are the limits on playing the game this way? Challenge pupils to record possible jumps with the different place value cards.

Optional adult input to groups

Extension: What number combinations are likely to pose difficulties?

Support: Point out that in each case up to the boundary only one part of the number changes.

Plenary

about 10 minutes

Key idea	We can count on and back in ones, tens and hundreds from any 2-digit or 3-digit number.

1. Discuss the different games. What numbers were recorded? What were the numbers they found most difficult to work with?
2. Ask children who made up sequences to challenge the rest of the class to work out what the relationship is.
3. Repeat the direct teaching counting activities as appropriate.

Homework suggestion

Starting with their street number count on 200, 500, 700 and 900.

Numbers 2.1 Odds and evens

Objectives
- count on from 0 or 1 in steps of 2 to about 50
- count on or back in steps of 2 starting from any 2-digit number
- recognise odd and even numbers to at least 100
- test whether a 2-digit number is odd or even

Key idea	A number that has 0, 2, 4, 6 or 8 as its units digit is even. A number that has 1, 3, 5, 7 or 9 as its units digit is odd.

Teaching model

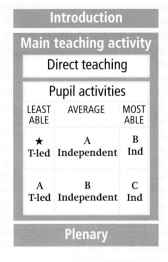

Introduction		
Main teaching activity		
Direct teaching		
Pupil activities		
LEAST ABLE	AVERAGE	MOST ABLE
★ T-led	A Independent	B Ind
A T-led	B Independent	C Ind
Plenary		

Key words count, odd, even, sequence, continue

You need

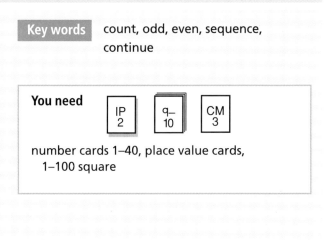

IP 2   9–10   CM 3

number cards 1–40, place value cards, 1–100 square

Introduction: oral work and mental calculation

about 5 minutes
Count on and back in steps of 2 starting from 0, and then from 1, to about 50.

Main teaching input and pupil activities

Direct teaching

about 20 minutes
1. Use IP 2. *Let's hang the wet socks on the washing line, one pair at a time. How many socks make a pair?*
2. Draw on giant pegs at 43 and 68. *All the socks from here (43) to here (68) are now dry. Let's say the numbers as we take the pairs off the line. 68, 66, ...* Children lower both hands for each step as if unpegging pairs of dry socks.
   Draw the giant pegs in other positions to practise counting on and back in 2s.
3. Draw a giant peg at 6. *How many children can have a pair of socks?* Repeat at 10 and 8. Now place a peg at 9. *How many children can have a*

pair of socks? Are there any socks left over? I have one sock left over because 9 is an odd number. What other numbers from 1 to 10 will leave us with an odd sock when we make pairs of socks? (1, 3, 5, 7) So we call 1, 3, 5, 7 and 9 odd numbers. Write them in a line.

What numbers from 1 to 10 will give us pairs of socks? (2, 4, 6, 8, 10) That's because 2, 4, 6, 8 and 10 are even numbers. Write them in a line next to the odd numbers.

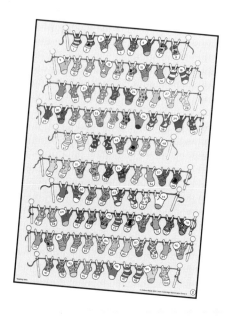

4. Choose about 12 socks numbered between 30 and 100 and ending in different units, for example: 53, 82, 79, 60, ... Ask children to work in pairs and test whether the numbers are odd or even. They could use bricks, count, make tallies, ...

5. Go through the numbers and ask children to tell you what they have found. Write the number in a column under its units digit or 10 (written up in 3 above) as appropriate. *What do you notice about the units digits in all the even numbers? ... the odd numbers?*

6. Point to random 2-digit numbers on a 100 square which children identify as even/odd by their units digit.

7. Circle 43, 45, 47 on the washing line. *Are they odd or even? What's the next odd number? And the next? Can you continue to 57?* Repeat several times with different sequences of odd and even numbers to at least 100. Repeat with sequences in descending order, with odd then even numbers.

Pupil activities

about 15 minutes
CORE   Independent
A TB page 9
Identify odd and even numbers.
B TB page 10
Find the odd/even number coming before/after, and continue sequences of odd/even numbers.
SUPPORT ★ Teacher-led
In pairs, children sort number cards 1–40 into sets of odd and even numbers. They make subsets of odd/even cards with the same units digit.
EXTENSION C Independent   CM 3
Children investigate positions of odd and even numbers and patterns of units digits in a 1–40 grid.

Optional adult input
Core: Help children to identify whether a number is odd or even by looking at the units digit.

Plenary

about 10 minutes

Key idea	A number that has 0, 2, 4, 6 or 8 as its units digit is even. A number that has 1, 3, 5, 7 or 9 as its units digit is odd.

1. Choose a tens and a units place value card. *The numbers are 20 and 5. Make me a 2-digit number... Is 25 odd or even? Can you point to 25 in the 100 square? In which units column is 25? Which number is 2 more/less than 25? Will that number be odd/even? How do you know? How could we test it?*

2. Repeat with other numbers.

Homework suggestion
Children investigate the pattern of odd/even numbers in a one-month calendar page.

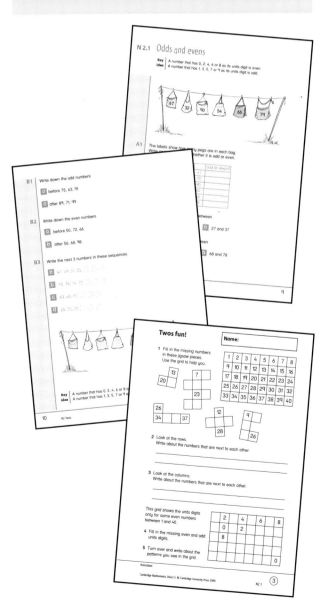

Numbers 2.2 Adding and subtracting odds and evens

Objectives
- make a general statement about odd and even numbers by finding examples that satisfy it
- investigate the sums and differences of pairs of odd and even numbers
- make a general statement about combining odd and even numbers by finding examples that satisfy it

Key idea If you add two even numbers the answer is even. If you add two odd numbers the answer is also even.

Teaching model

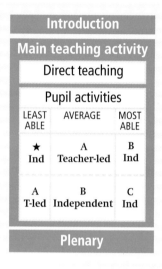

Introduction
Main teaching activity
Direct teaching
Pupil activities

LEAST ABLE	AVERAGE	MOST ABLE
★ Ind	A Teacher-led	B Ind
A T-led	B Independent	C Ind

Plenary

Key words count, how many?, odd, even, sequence

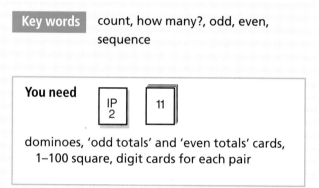

You need IP 2 | 11
dominoes, 'odd totals' and 'even totals' cards, 1–100 square, digit cards for each pair

Introduction: oral work and mental calculation

about 5 minutes

1. Use IP 2. Ask a child to point to a sock with a hole.
   Look at the number on the sock. Is it odd or even?
   Repeat for all the socks with holes.
2. *How many socks have holes? Let's count. Is the total an odd or an even number? How do you know?*
3. *What are the next 3 odd/even numbers after 51/47/96, ...?*
   What are the 3 odd/even numbers before 63/72/94/80, ...?

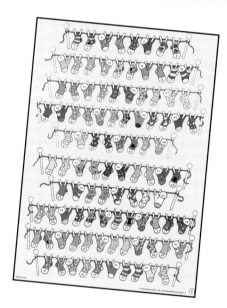

Main teaching input and pupil activities

Direct teaching

about 20 minutes

1. Use IP 2. Ask a child to count the pegs along a washing line stopping at the sixth peg. Write 6 in red on the peg.
   Let's suppose your fingers are the pegs. Is 6 odd or even? Is 4 odd or even? Let's add these two even numbers 4

and 6. Will the answer be an odd or an even number? Check with your fingers.
Write 10 in red on the tenth peg.
What if we add another 5 pegs? Will the answer be odd or even? How do you know?
Write 15 in blue on the fifteenth peg.

2. Repeat with other starting numbers up to 20, adding on odd and even numbers of pegs and writing the numbers on the pegs in red (evens) or blue (odds).

3. Use these numbered and coloured pegs to investigate pairs of numbers that produce odd and even totals, for example:

   The answer is 12. What pairs of even numbers can you add to make 12?

   The answer is 12. What pairs of odd numbers can you add to make 12?

   If I add any 2 even/odd numbers, will the answer be odd or even? Give me some examples with 2-digit numbers.

4. Investigate the differences of pairs of odd and even numbered pegs. If possible, extend to numbers beyond 20.

Pupil activities

about 15 minutes

CORE

A Teacher-led TB page 11

Children find the sums of pairs of even numbers and differences of pairs of odd numbers. Encourage children to find at least 6 different answers in questions 1 and 3.

B Independent TB page 11

Children need digit cards 1–9. You may wish to pair children for this activity.

SUPPORT ★ Independent

Provide each small group with a set of dominoes and 2 label cards, 'even totals', 'odd totals'. Extract the 7 tiles which have blanks.

The children shuffle the dominoes face down on the table. In turn, they lift a tile, add the spots from each half of the domino and sort the tile. Discuss the tiles in the 'even totals' set.

EXTENSION C Independent

Children test the statement, 'You can make any even number by adding 2 odd numbers.' They list all the possible odd number combinations for 30. Then they investigate the sums of pairs of odd 2-digit numbers.

Optional adult input

Support: Check that children are adding the numbers on the dominoes rather than just counting them.

Extension: Encourage children to record systematically and to think of all the combinations they can.

Plenary

about 10 minutes

Key idea	If you add two even numbers the answer is even. If you add two odd numbers the answer is also even.

1. Review the work from the textbook. Ask some children to tell the class which numbers they combined for the addition and subtraction sentences.

   What is the largest even total you could make? The greatest difference?

2. If you subtract an even number from an even number, will the answer be odd or even?

   Give me some examples from the 100 square.

3. Compare and discuss some of the possible arrangements for the number cards in the puzzle.

   Where must you place the even cards? Why?

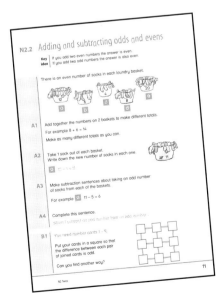

Homework suggestion

Find a pack of playing cards and remove the picture cards. Play 'Odd and even snap'.

Numbers 2.3 What if?

Objectives
- investigate what even totals can be made using three 1–6 dice
- explore ways of making even numbers up to 20 as the sum of four 1-digit odd numbers
- suggest extensions by asking 'What if?'

Key idea | When we ask ourselves 'What if?' we make up interesting questions to answer.

Teaching model

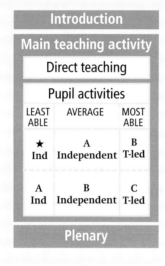

Key words odd, even, greatest, least

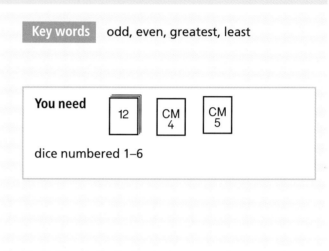

Introduction: oral work and mental calculation

about 5 minutes

1. Play 'Elimination':
   Children stand up and each choose a 2-digit number.
   Sit down if:
   your number is odd (even);
   your number is a multiple of 10 (or 5);
   the tens digit is greater (or less) than the units digit;
   the sum of the digits is more than (or less than) 10;
   the units digit is 1 (or 2, 3, ... 9).
   Continue until all are eliminated but one, the winner.
   Repeat several times, adjusting the conditions.

Main teaching input and pupil activities

Direct teaching

about 15 minutes

1. Briefly discuss the commutative property of addition. Demonstrate that, for example, 4 + 2 gives the same answer as 2 + 4.
2. Compare and talk about trios of 1-digit numbers. Establish that 2 + 2 + 4 is the same as 2 + 4 + 2 and 4 + 2 + 2 by rearranging the order of three dice showing these numbers.
3. *Can we make a total of 2 with 3 dice? What is the lowest even total I can make with 3 dice?* (4) *What are the 3 numbers?* (1, 1, and 2)
   It is important that children begin to learn the strategies of listing and working systematically so on the board draw a table with 4 columns:

even total	dice 1	dice 2	dice 3
4	1	1	2

4. *What's the next even total we can make?* (6) *Tell me a way we can make 6. Is there another way?* (1, 1 and 4 or 2, 2 and 2) Write the solutions in the table.
5. *What even number comes after 6? Can we make 8 if we begin with 2 ones? Are there other ways to make 8?*
   Write the solutions in the table.
6. *What's the greatest total we can make with 3 dice?* (18)
7. *What if the dice were numbered from 5 to 10? What is the lowest even total you can make?* (16) *The greatest?* (30)

Pupil activities

about 15 minutes

CORE   Independent TB page 12

A The recording of the even totals will give children practice in listing.

B This activity follows on from A and so is teacher-led for the most able children, if you do not want them to complete A first. Children explore ways of making even numbers up to 20 as the sum of 4 odd 1-digit numbers. They use listing skills and work systematically through the task.

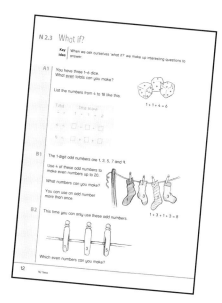

SUPPORT ★ Independent   CM 4
Children find what even totals they can make with 2 dice and record on the grid.
EXTENSION C Teacher-led   CM 5

Optional adult input
Core: Encourage children to consider whether they have found all the possible combinations.

Plenary

about 10 minutes

Key idea	When we ask ourselves 'What if?' we make up interesting questions to answer.

1. Ask children who did the support activity to talk about what happens when you add two numbers that are the same.
2. Discuss ways children found of making 12 as the sum of four 1-digit odd numbers (B1). *What if you only use the odd numbers 1, 3 and 5? How many ways can you make 12? (3)*
3. Compare and discuss some of the ways to make 20 using odd numbers.
4. *What if we make the rule 'The first 2 numbers are even and the same'. Tell me some of the ways we can make 20 as the sum of four 1-digit numbers.*

Homework
You have 4 coins in your pocket and their total is even.
The highest-value coin is a 5p.
What even sums of money might you have?

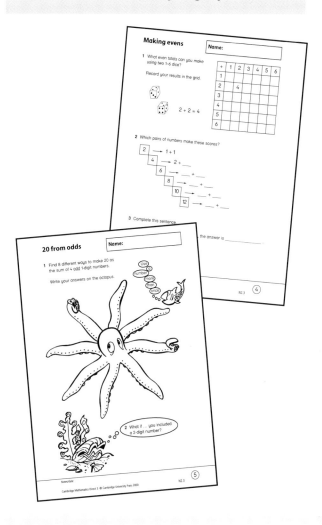

Numbers 3.1 Steps of 2, 3, 4 and 5

Objectives
- count on in steps of 2, 3, 4, 5, 10 or 100 from any small number, then back again
- describe sequences and extend them

Key idea	We can count on and back in steps of 2, 3, 4, 5, 10 or 100 from any small number.

Teaching model

Introduction

Main teaching activity
Direct teaching

Pupil activities		
LEAST ABLE	AVERAGE	MOST ABLE
★ T-led	A Independent	B Ind
A T-led	B Independent	C Ind

Plenary

Key words sequence, continue, rule, relationship

You need

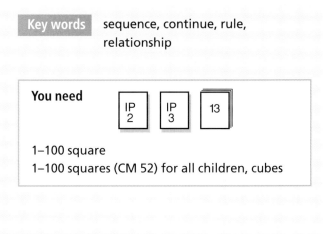

IP 2   IP 3   13

1–100 square
1–100 squares (CM 52) for all children, cubes

Introduction: oral work and mental calculation

about 5 minutes

Make 2 large groups. Group 1 counts forwards. Group 2 counts backwards. Group 1 starts counting on in 10s from any single-digit number. When you clap your hands, Group 2 counts backwards. The direction of the count changes every time you clap.

Repeat the activity for steps of 2, 3, 4 or 5 to 30.

Main teaching input and pupil activities

Direct teaching

about 25 minutes

1. Play 'Mechanical maze' on IP 3 (see page 14).
2. Discuss the position of numbers ending in 5 and 0 on IP 2 and on the 1–100 square. Draw children's attention to the patterns. *How many steps is it from 25 to 30? From 65 to 70?*

3. Count in 5s from 2 to 52 on the 1–100 square. Write 2, 7, 12, 17, 22 on the board. *What are the next 2 numbers in this sequence? How many steps from 17 to 22? From 22 to 27?*

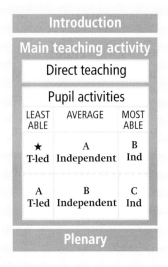

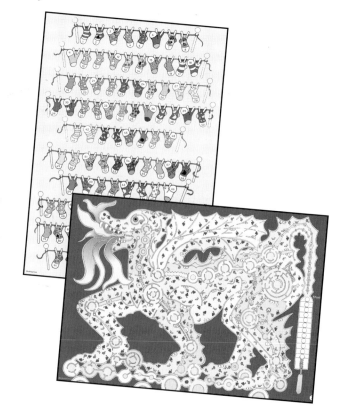

4. Working in pairs, children choose a small number and place a cube on it on their 1–100 square. Counting on in 5s, they place a cube on every fifth number up to 50.

5. Discuss the cube patterns and the relationship between cubes in the same row. Invite children to select 4 numbers in sequence from their 1–100 square. Ask the class to give the next 2 numbers in the sequence. *Explain how you worked out what would come next.*

6. Repeat for steps of 4, but this time start at a number between 40 and 50 and count back.

7. Write 5, 9, 13 on the board. *Who can describe this sequence? What would the next number be? What would the number before the 5 be? How did you work it out?* (By working out what the step was between the numbers, i.e. using the difference.)

Pupil activities

about 15 minutes

CORE Independent

A Children make up a sequence with cubes on their 1–100 squares, counting in the step of their choice from any small number. They write down 4 consecutive numbers in the sequence. Children swap sequences with a partner and write the next 4 numbers in the sequence.

B Independent TB page 13

Children complete sequences.

SUPPORT ★ Teacher-led

Ask children to put cubes on 1, 4 and 7. What is the pattern? How can they work out what comes next? Repeat for other sequences.

EXTENSION C Independent TB page 13

Children make up their own sequences.

Optional adult input to groups

Core: Encourage children to find the difference between consecutive numbers and to check by looking at other numbers.

Extension: Can children use what they notice about the units digits to help them predict what will come next in the sequence?

Plenary

about 10 minutes

Key idea	We can count on and back in steps of 2, 3, 4, 5, 10 or 100 from any small number.

1. Ask children to remind one another how to work out what the next number in a sequence is.

2. Ask those children who completed B to explain what they did. *Which were the hardest questions? What do you need to know in order to fill in the missing gaps? What if you only had a starting/ finishing number, could you work out what the other numbers in the sequence are?*

3. What did the extension children find out about the units digits in their sequences?

4. Play 'Mechanical maze' on IP 3 (see page 14).

Homework suggestion

Look at the calendar for this month. Choose your favourite day of the week. What dates are these days? Write these 4 (5) dates in order and find the next 2 numbers in the sequence.

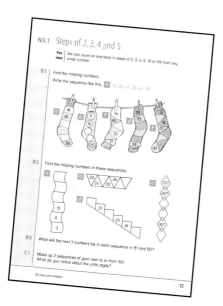

Numbers 3.2 Making patterns by counting

Objectives
- describe and continue sequences formed by counting on and back in steps of 2, 3, 4 or 5 in a 5 × 5 square and extend to a 6 × 6 square.
- create sequences with a given constraint

Key idea	When you want to describe a sequence, look for the pattern first and then use the pattern to make the rule.

Teaching model

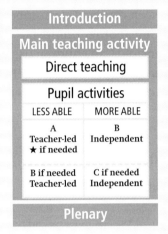

Key words   count, sequence, continue, rule

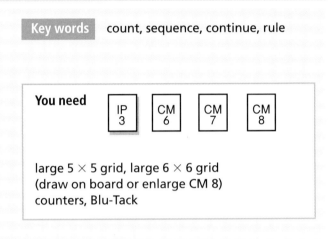

large 5 × 5 grid, large 6 × 6 grid
(draw on board or enlarge CM 8)
counters, Blu-Tack

Introduction: oral work and mental calculation

about 5 minutes
Play 'Mechanical maze' on IP 3 (see page 14).

Main teaching input and pupil activities

Direct teaching

about 15 minutes

1. Use CM 8. Ask children to cover the numbers 1, 6 and 11 on a 5 × 5 grid with counters. *Who can describe the pattern? What is the rule? Who can continue it? Will 29 be in this sequence? Will 42? How do you know?*

2. *If we started at 3, would the pattern be the same?*

3. Repeat for another step.

4. Ask a child to pick 2 numbers between 8 and 15, e.g 10 and 14. *If these are numbers in a sequence, what is the number before 10? What is the number after 14?*

5. Ask children to make up a sequence which uses 9 and 17. Compare their examples. They

are most likely to come up with 1, 9, 17, 25, which uses the difference between 9 and 17. 1, 5, 9, 13, 17, 21, 25 and 1, 3, 5, 7, 9, 11, 13, 15, 17, 19, 21, 23, 25 are also possible.

6. Ask children to create a sequence with a given constraint, e.g with the numbers 8 and 17 in it.

Pupil activities

about 20 minutes

LESS ABLE Teacher-led   CM 6 and 8
CORE A

Children record and describe sequences on a
5 × 5 grid and make up their own with a given
rule. They can move on to a 6 × 6 grid when they
are ready.

SUPPORT ★

Before photocopying CM6, ring the numbers in
the sequence for questions 1 and 3.

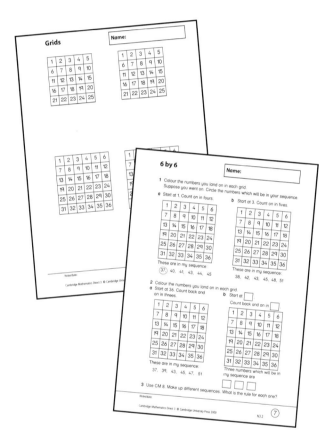

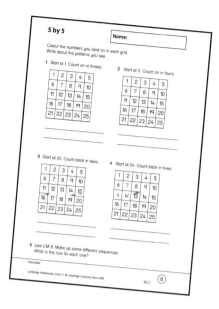

Plenary

about 10 minutes

Key idea	When you want to describe a sequence, look for the pattern first and then use the pattern to make the rule.

1. Ask children to display their patterns. *If you
   continued your sequence, would 29 be in it? How do
   you know? What would happen if you started at 4
   instead of 6, would the pattern be the same?*
2. Ask children what they notice about the
   patterns of the units digits.

Homework suggestion

Give children a copy of CM 8 and ask them to
work out two patterns for someone at home to
describe and continue.

MORE ABLE Independent   CM 7 and 8
CORE B

Children record and describe sequences on a
6 × 6 grid and then make up rules of their own
and sequences to satisfy them.

EXTENSION C

Children make a number of 6 × 10 grids on
squared paper and extend the patterns beyond 36
to 60. What do they notice?

Optional adult input to groups

More able: Encourage children to work out
patterns that they think no-one else will come up
with.

Numbers 3.3 Multiples of 2, 5 and 10

Objectives	• use the term multiple
	• recognise 2- and 3-digit multiples of 2, 5 and 10
	• recognise that multiples of 10 are also multiples of 5

Key idea	We can tell if a 2- or 3-digit number is a multiple of 2, 5 or 10 by looking at the last digit.

Teaching model

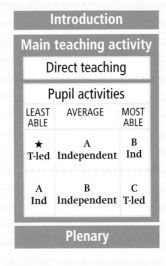

Key words   sequence, multiple, predict, continue

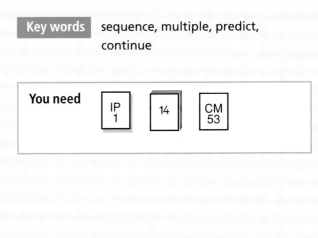

Introduction: oral work and mental calculation

about 5 minutes

Count on and back in steps of 2, 5 and 10 from 0 and 2- and 3-digit numbers.

Main teaching input and pupil activities

Direct teaching

about 15 minutes

1. Use IP 1. Count on in 2s from zero, marking each square you land on. List the units digits of the numbers. *Who can see a pattern? Who can say the pattern? ... predict what will come after 100?*

2. Link counting on in 2s to the 2 times-table. Remind children that the 'multiple' of a number is any answer in the times-table for that number. *So all these numbers we have marked on here are multiples of 2. What can you tell me about the last digit of all the multiples of 2 that are on this 0–100 grid? Is this true for numbers up to 200?*

3. Ask children to work with a partner to test out what happens to 3-digit multiples of 2 and also to investigate multiples of 5 and 10.

4. Ask children to share their results. Build up and write on the board:

multiples of 10	end in 0
multiples of 5	end in 0 or 5
multiples of 2	end in 0, 2, 4, 6 or 8

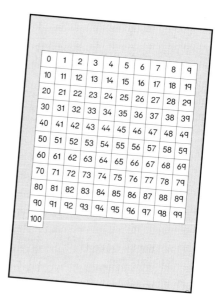

Pupil activities

about 20 minutes
CORE   Independent   TB page 14
A and **B** Children identify 2-digit and 3-digit multiples of 2, 5 and 10.

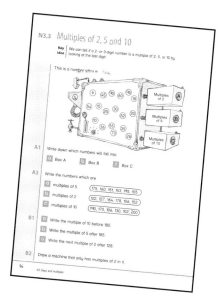

SUPPORT ★ Teacher-led CM 53
Children count on in steps of 5 from 0 on CM 53 and mark the multiples of 5. They colour the entries in each line in the same colour, to bring out the 0, 5 endings. Repeat for multiples of 2 on a new 0–100 grid.

EXTENSION C Teacher-led CM 53
On CM 53 children colour yellow multiples of 2 and blue multiples of 5. What can they say about the numbers that turn out green?

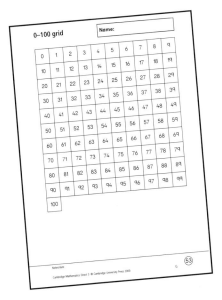

Optional adult input to groups
Core: Help children to focus on the last digit of each number.
Support: Encourage children to pick out the repeating pattern of the final digits.

Plenary

about 10 minutes

Key idea	We can tell if a 2- or 3-digit number is a multiple of 2, 5 or 10 by looking at the last digit.

1. Ask children to describe to their neighbour what a multiple of 2 looks like. Repeat for multiples of 5 and 10.
2. Invite children to suggest a number and to ask the class to say what it is a multiple of. They can also ask trick questions with numbers that are not multiples of 2, 5 or 10 or that are multiples of all three.
3. What did the extension group find out about numbers which are multiples of both 2 and 5? Can they explain why this should be so?
4. Ask the support group to talk about the pattern of multiples and how they can be used to work out what number comes next in that times-table.

Homework suggestion
Children work out how many 2p and 5p coins they need for each multiple of 10p up to £1. Can they see a pattern in the answers?

Numbers 3.4 Multiples of 50 and 100

Objectives
- count in 50s to 1000
- recognise 3-digit multiples of 50 and 100
- recognise that multiples of 100 are also multiples of 50

Key idea	We can count in steps of 50 and 100.

Teaching model

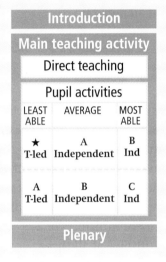

Key words count, multiple, sequence

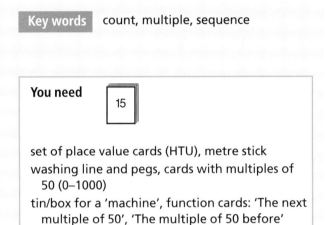

You need

set of place value cards (HTU), metre stick
washing line and pegs, cards with multiples of 50 (0–1000)
tin/box for a 'machine', function cards: 'The next multiple of 50', 'The multiple of 50 before'

Introduction: oral work and mental calculation

about 5 minutes

Ask:

What is the first multiple of 2/5/10 after 101?

Where will we find all the multiples of 10/5?

Tell me a multiple of 2/5/10 less than 140 / more than 180.

What is the next multiple of 10/5 before/after 175?

Main teaching input and pupil activities

Direct teaching

about 20 minutes

1. Hold up the blank face of a metre stick. Point to the middle of the stick and say:
   The ends of my stick are zero and 10. What number is halfway along the stick?
   The ends of my stick are zero and 100/1000. What number is midway between zero and 100/1000?

2. Draw a number line on the board. Through discussion build up this diagram:

0	5	10
0	50	100
0	500	1000

   Draw children's attention to the 2 equal jumps of 5/50/500 making 10/100/1000.

3. Peg the cards 0 and 1000 on the washing line. Distribute the remaining cards (50–950) to individual children. Ask the children holding 'multiple of 100' cards to make a line so that the person to their left is holding a 'hundred more' card. When they are all in place the class counts in 100s from 0. Children peg their 'multiple of 100' cards on the line.

4. Ask questions that will focus on the place value of the remaining cards, e.g.
   Who has the 150 card? Where will you hang it on the line?
   Who has the card that comes between 600 and 700?
   Who has the card that is 50 more/less than 200?

5. Use the filled washing line to count in 50s to 1000, then back again.Children close their eyes as you remove a card from the line, and adjust the space! *Which card is missing?*

6. Use the large box and the cards from the washing line for a 'function machine' game. A tin of drawing pins can add a 'mechanical' touch when shaken.
   I put this card (hold up 250) *into the machine* (shake the tin) *and this card comes out* (hold up 300).
   Repeat the process for 3 more cards.
   I'm putting 650 into the machine. Who can tell me the number that will come out?
   What is the machine doing to the cards? (jumping on to the next multiple of 50)
   Place the correct function card on the front of the box.

Pupil activities

about 15 minutes

CORE   Independent   TB page 15
A and B Children practise recognising and generating multiples of 50 and 100.

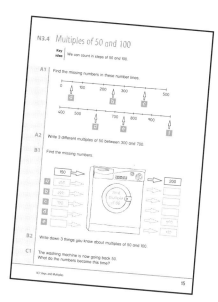

SUPPORT ★ Teacher-led
Repeat the washing line activity.
EXTENSION C Independent   TB page 15
Children play machine activity where the function is 'multiple of 50 before'.

Optional adult input to groups
Core: Help children to see the connection between counting in 50s and counting in 5s.
Extension: What if it were 150 before?

Plenary

about 10 minutes

Key idea	We can count in steps of 50 and 100.

1. Support children set problems on the washing line for the class to solve.

2. Discuss the facts that children know about multiples of 50 and 100. Build up and write on the board, taking care to align the columns:

multiples of	2	end in	0, 2, 4, 6, 8
multiples of	5	end in	0 or 5
multiples of	10	end in	0
multiples of	50	end in	00 or 50
multiples of	100	end in	00

Highlight the relationship between multiples of 5 and 10, and between multiples of 50 and 100, in terms of place value.

3. Hold up place value cards showing a 3-digit number. *Is this a multiple of 5, ... 2, ... 10, ... 50?*

4. Invite a child to choose the numbers.

Homework suggestion
You have five £1 coins and ten 50p coins. What different amounts can you make?

Numbers 4.1 Dice and dominoes

Objectives
- solve number puzzles and problems
- recognise simple patterns and relationships
- make predictions about patterns and begin to identify a general pattern

Key idea	Knowing a pattern can help us predict the answer to a problem.

Teaching model

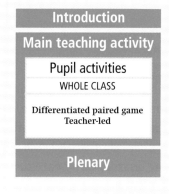

Key words odd, even, predict, pattern, total

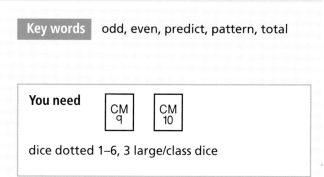

Introduction: oral work and mental calculation

about 5 minutes

Play 'Fingers':

Split the class into 2 teams: Evens and Odds. Choose 4 children. On a given signal, they each quickly hold up a number of fingers on one hand. Total the numbers shown. If total is odd (even), Odds (Evens) win a point, e.g. if 2, 3, 4 and 5 are shown, the total is 14, so Evens win a point.

Main teaching input and pupil activities

Direct teaching

about 15 minutes

1. Tell children that they will be trying to make odd and even numbers and using patterns to predict whether they can or not.
2. Roll 2 large dice. *You win a point if you can make an odd number. You can decide whether to add or subtract the numbers. Can we make an odd number with these scores? Were the numbers we started with odd or even?* Record the calculations on the board and whether the starting numbers were

odd or even. Repeat. (Later in the lesson, children will discover that it is only possible to make an odd number when working with 2 numbers if one is odd and one even.)

3. Repeat the game using 3 dice. Show children that there are several ways to order the scores. *Can you arrange the numbers in a different way? Would it help if you subtracted one of the numbers?* Record the calculations on the board and repeat. (Children will discover later that it is only possible to make an odd number when working with a set of numbers that contains an odd number of odd numbers.)

Pupil activities

about 20 minutes
CORE   Teacher-led   CM 9
Paired game

In pairs, children repeat the Direct teaching activity with 3 dice. They record the calculations that they make and whether the answers are odd or even. They look for a pattern in their results. How can this pattern help them to predict whether they can make an odd number just by looking at the scores they have thrown?

SUPPORT   Independent   CM 10

In pairs, children take it in turns to throw 2 dice and add the scores. What can they say about the pairs of numbers that make an odd total?

EXTENSION   Independent

Children repeat the Direct teaching activity with 4 or more dice. What patterns can they see?

Optional adult input to groups

Support: Check that children identify the 2 numbers they throw rather than count the spots. Extension: Encourage children to investigate the number of odd and even numbers they work with.

Plenary

about 10 minutes

Key idea	Knowing a pattern can help us predict the answer to a problem.

1. Ask children who did the support activity to describe what they did and found out.
2. Ask the class, *If you throw 3 dice, can you predict whether you will be able to make an odd or an even number? How do you know?*
3. Ask the extension group to talk about what they found out. How can we use this pattern?

Homework suggestion
Play 'Fingers' at home and record the results.

Numbers 4.2 Puzzles and problems

Objectives ● use cubes and number cards to solve number puzzles and problems
● extend problems by asking 'What if …?'
● make and test predictions

Key idea	We can solve a puzzle and then change it by asking 'What if …?'

Teaching model

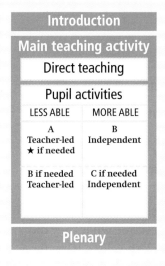

Key words   add, subtract, equals, check, equation, operation, how many?

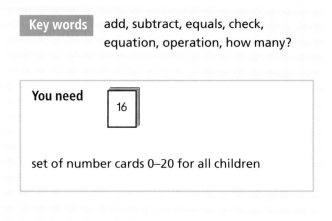

You need   16

set of number cards 0–20 for all children

Introduction: oral work and mental calculation

about 5 minutes

Work out 3 + 4, 6 + 1 + 5, 9 − 5 + 2, … Work up to combining 4 numbers. Ensure that all children have made an answer before asking them to hold up their number cards.

Main teaching input and pupil activities

Direct teaching

about 15 minutes

1. Explain that an equation has 2 sides that are equal or balance. We put an equals sign between the 2 sides to show that they are equal. Show the children a few examples:
   5 + 2 = 8 − 1, 8 = 5 + 1 + 2.
   Using those numbers, can you show me another example? (8 − 5 − 1 = 2, 8 − 5 − 2 = 1, 8 − 2 − 1 = 5, 8 − 2 = 5 + 1, 8 − 5 = 2 + 1)

2. *We are going to use numbers and add or subtract them to make equations. We are going to try to find as many different equations as possible.* Ask for another example of the type of equation you have just been looking at. *How do we choose the numbers?* Work through it with the children.

Pupil activities

about 20 minutes
LESS ABLE   Teacher-led
CORE A
Give children another set of 4 numbers: 9, 4, 2 and 3. Ask them to predict how many equations they will be able to make and give a reason for their prediction. Encourage them to work systematically as they record different equations. How do they know they have found all they can?
SUPPORT ★
How many different equations can you find using these 3 numbers: 7, 3 and 4? (3)

MORE ABLE   Independent   TB page 16
CORE B
Children choose 4 numbers for themselves and
record the different equations that are possible.
Then they ask 'What if ...?'
EXTENSION C
What if we use 5 different numbers: 1, 3, 9, 5 and 2?
How many equations do you think we can make
now? (11)

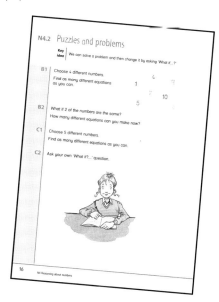

Optional adult input to groups
Support: Encourage children to work
systematically. Ensure that they are working out
the answers rather than moving the numbers
around.
Extension: Ask them to show how they know they
have all the different equations.

Plenary

about 10 minutes

Key idea	We can solve a puzzle and then change it by asking 'What if ...?'

1. Ask children to show the equations they made.
   How many equations could we make with 3
   numbers? ... 4 numbers? ... 5 numbers?
2. Ask children to explain their systems for
   tackling and recording the problem.
3. *Was your prediction correct?*
4. *Do you think the number of numbers you choose*
   affects the number of equations you can make?
5. Talk about the 'What if ...' question. What
   other questions could they ask?

Homework suggestion
Use the numbers 1, 2, 3 and 6 to make as many
equations as you can.

Numbers 4.3 Grids

Objectives • solve number puzzles and problems that require square and triangular grid
arrangements
• use trial and improvement strategies
• develop logical reasoning skills
• explain methods and reasoning about numbers orally and in writing

**Key
idea**   Sometimes, seeing a pattern helps us solve problems or puzzles.

Teaching model

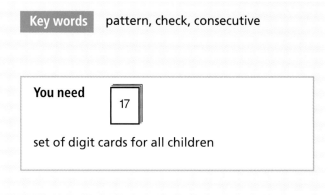

Key words   pattern, check, consecutive

You need

17

set of digit cards for all children

Introduction: oral work and mental calculation

about 5 minutes
*Show me the next number in this pattern: 12, 10, 8, 6, ...
110, 107, 104, 101, ...*
Ask children to describe the patterns and explain
how they worked out what number would come
next.

Main teaching input and pupil activities

Direct teaching

about 15 minutes
1. Tell the children that they will be solving
   puzzles that all contain adding patterns. *Look
   out for the patterns because finding a pattern helps
   in solving the puzzle.*
2. Draw on the board a triangle with 6 boxes, one
   box at each corner and one in the middle of
   each side. *When we put the numbers 1–6 in the
   boxes, we want each side of the triangle to add up to
   12. Who could have a go at telling me where we
   might put some of the numbers? Try possibilities
   with the class.*

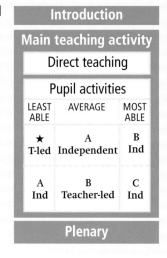

3. *How can we check that each side is the same?*
   Encourage children to demonstrate,
   addressing any misconceptions that become
   apparent.

Pupil activities

about 20 minutes

CORE

A Independent   TB page 17

Children use digit cards 1–6 to make a triangle with sides that each total 9.

B Teacher-led

The most able children may complete this activity independently.

Using all the digit cards, can you make triangles with sides that all equal another amount? Children record their solutions on paper. *Can you see a pattern that helps you to solve other triangle puzzles?*

SUPPORT ★ Teacher-led TB page 17

Children check the triangles to find which have sides that each add up to the same number.

EXTENSION C Independent   TB page 17

Children choose their own 6 consecutive numbers to make a 'magic' triangle.

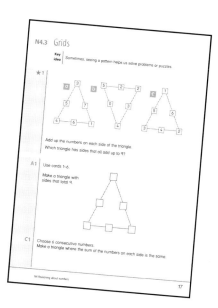

Optional adult input to groups

Less able: Ask how they can check that all the sides add up to the same amount.

Plenary

about 10 minutes

| **Key idea** | Sometimes, seeing a pattern helps us solve problems or puzzles. |

1. Ask children to show the triangles they found (support) or made with sides that are equal. *How can we check that the sides all add up to the same number?*
2. *After you had made the triangle with 9 on each side, did you begin to see a pattern? Were you able to use that pattern to help you make another triangle with sides that have the same total?*
3. Ask the extension group to explain what they did.
4. *What if we use this set of consecutive numbers: 6, 7, 8, 9, 10, 11? Can anyone see a quick way of arranging them so that the sides are of equal value?*

Homework suggestion

Arrange the numbers 0–5 on a triangle so that the total of each side is 6.

Numbers 4.4 Repeating patterns

Objectives • identify and create patterns of multiples
• investigate a general statement about familiar numbers
• explain methods and reasoning about numbers orally and in writing

Key idea	Being able to spot patterns and talk about them can help you solve lots of number problems.

Teaching model

Introduction

Main teaching activity
Direct teaching

Pupil activities		
LEAST ABLE	AVERAGE	MOST ABLE
★ T-led	A Independent	B Ind
A T-led	B Independent	C Ind

Plenary

Key words pattern, sequence, predict, continue, multiple

You need

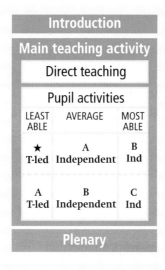

IP 3 | 18 | CM 11 | CM 12

counting stick, cubes, small cards and Blu-Tack for covering up numbers on the board, counters

Introduction: oral work and mental calculation

about 5 minutes

1. Make sticks of cubes, e.g. 2 red, 2 yellow, 2 red, 2 yellow, ... Use these to aid the quick recall of patterns of known multiples.
2. Count multiples along the stick: 0, 2, 4, 6, ... Ask children to continue the pattern. Try multiples of other numbers, such as 5, 10, 4, ...

Main teaching input and pupil activities

Direct teaching

about 15 minutes

1. *This lesson is about finding number sequences just like we did on the counting stick. This time the sequence might not be part of a multiplication table. During this lesson, I want you to look for number patterns and try to describe them to me or someone else.*
2. Draw an array of the numbers 1–10 in 2 rows on the board. Explain that the numbers are in a pattern. *Can you describe any of the patterns in the array?* (Each number is 1 more than the

number on its left; each number is 5 less than the number below it, ...)
3. Now draw up an array using the multiples of 10 up to 100 in two adjacent columns. Ask the children to describe the pattern. Cover up one of the numbers. *Can you work out which number I've hidden?* Before uncovering the number, ask the child to give a reason based on their knowledge of the pattern. If they predict correctly, the class wins a counter; if not, you win one.

Pupil activities

about 20 minutes
CORE

A Independent TB page 18

In pairs, children describe the patterns in the arrays to each other and write their explanations down. They play 'What's that number?' on each one, using counters to hide numbers.

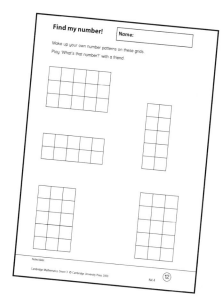

B Independent CM 12

Children make up their own patterns on the blank grids.

SUPPORT ★ Teacher-led CM 11

Look at the arrays on the copymaster and work out the missing numbers. *What patterns can you see that can help you complete the arrays?*

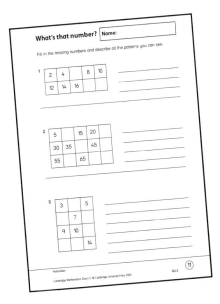

EXTENSION C Independent CM 12

Children check their friend's arrays to make sure that they really are in a pattern. They can then play on their own grids, hiding more and more numbers.

Optional adult input to groups

Core: Help children to identify the patterns on the arrays and then to use what they know to work out what the hidden numbers are.

Extension: Encourage children to try using patterns that are not just based on multiplication facts.

Plenary

about 10 minutes

Key idea	Being able to spot patterns and talk about them can help you solve lots of number problems.

1. Ask children to show the arrays they have made up. *Can you see the patterns?* Cover a number. *How could you work out what this number is?*
2. *If I said that one of the patterns in this array was part of the multiplication table for 3, would I be right?*
3. Play 'Mechanical maze' on IP 3 (see page 14).

Homework suggestion

Play 'What's that number?' at home.

Numbers 4.5 Extending patterns

Objectives • record and investigate steps of 2, 3, 4, 5, 10 between any 2-digit numbers, giving examples to match general statements

Key idea	If you can see patterns in numbers, you can sometimes win games.

Teaching model

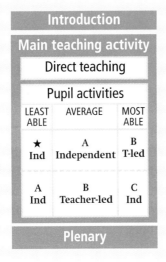

Key words odd, even, sequence, predict, continue, rule, relationship multiple

You need

IP 1 IP 3 19–20 CM 13 CM 14

counters, dice marked 2, 2, 3, 4, 5, 10

Introduction: oral work and mental calculation

about 10 minutes

1. Divide the class into 2 teams. Team A says the odd numbers and team B, the even numbers. Draw a circle on IP 1 to mark the starting number.
   Children count on in steps of 2, 3, 4, 5 and 10, then back to the starting number.
   Repeat with different 2-digit starting numbers.
2. Play 'Mechanical maze' on IP 3 (see page 14).

Main teaching input and pupil activities

Direct teaching

about 15 minutes

1. Discuss the patterns found in the starter activity, namely
   counting in 10s – same units digit
   counting in 5s – units digit alternates
   counting in 2s/4s
     – if starting number is even, all units even
     – if starting number is odd, all units odd
   counting in 3s – alternate odd and even units digits

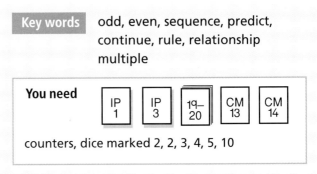

2. Provide pairs of children with a copy of CM 13 'Jumping frogs', 1 large and 12 small counters and a dice marked 2, 2, 3, 4, 5, 10.
   Discuss the rules for 'Jumping frogs'. Allow enough time for children to have several turns each.

3. Discuss the combinations of starting numbers and dice throws which produce winning jumps.
Are you more likely to land on 36 if you begin on an even number than an odd number? Why?
(2 appears twice on the dice)
Is 7 a 'lucky' starting number? Why not? (Jumps will not finish on 36)
My starting number is 4. Which numbers should I hope to throw with the dice? (2, 4)
What if my starting number is 3? Which number must I throw? (3)
I heard someone say, 'If my starting number is 6, I can't lose.' Is this a true statement? How do you know? Give me some examples of how it works for 6.
(All 6 faces 'win')

4. Briefly discuss the first few general statements on TB page 19.

Pupil activities

about 20 minutes

CORE

A Independent   TB page 19
These are closed questions for children to answer.

B Teacher-led   TB page 19–20
Children extend patterns to answer questions which are more open-ended.

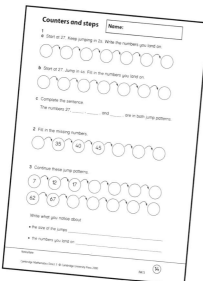

SUPPORT ★ Independent   CM 14
The use of jumping circles will help children become more confident counting on in steps from any number.

EXTENSION C Independent   TB page 20
Children play the 'Jumping frogs' game in 'reverse'. The starting numbers are between 30 and 36. The objective is to land exactly on zero.

Optional adult input to groups
Core: Ask children to describe the number patterns that are being produced.

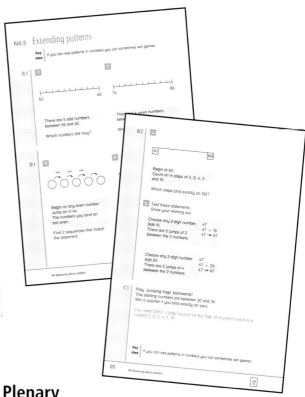

Plenary

about 10 minutes

| Key idea | If you can see patterns in numbers, you can sometimes win games. |

1. Review the textbook activities, with special attention to the tasks which children found more difficult.

2. Ask individual children to state the sequences they made for question B1.

3. Say to the children who completed B2b:
You found that there were 5 jumps of 4 between each pair of numbers. How many jumps of 2 will there be between the same pair of numbers?
What if the pairs of numbers were 3-digit numbers? Will you still have 5 jumps of 4?
Can you give us an example of this?

4. What did the extension group find out when they played 'Jumping frogs' in reverse? (The same facts are true as for the game played the other way round.)

Homework suggestion
Children take a copy of 'Jumping frogs' to play at home with an adult. Keep a record of turns.

Glossary

Key words and terms to be used with children

units or ones, tens, hundreds, numeral, digit, 1-, 2-, 3-digit number, place value, first, second, third, fourth, ..., more than, less than, fewer than, greater than, smaller than, larger than, smallest, largest, order, position, last, before, after, next, how many?, as many as, equal to, between, half way, difference between, thousand, zero, odd, even, measuring scale, division

digit a numeral consists of one or more digits

ordinal number the numerical position in a series, e.g. first, second, third

place value describes the value of a digit in a number in our number system

General overview of the topic

The way we write numbers derives from the Indo-Arabic number system and is based on a system of grouping in tens. Any number, however great or small, can be expressed using only the ten different digits.

In any number, each digit has a specific value defined by its position. When discussing parts of a number it is important to refer to 'digits' rather than to 'numbers', e.g. when asking what the value of 6 is in 263, ask about 'the digit 6' rather than 'the number 6'.

Children use their understanding of place value when comparing or ordering numbers with more than one digit and when reading scales.

Place value 1: Understanding place value
Children extend their understanding of place value to 3 digits and look at what happens when they add or subtract 1, 10 or 100.

Place value 2: Exploring place value
Children use their understanding of the number system to compare and order numbers and measures.

Place value 3: Using place value
Place value is applied further to ordering and comparing numbers and measures, and reading scales.

Links between blocks

Place value 1 revises what children know about 2-digit numbers and extends this to numbers to 500. It therefore makes a good start to the year. Place value 2 and 3 then develop these ideas and could be taught in successive terms.

Before they start, children need to

- understand place value in numbers to 100
- know the value of digits in a 2-digit number
- recognise zero as a place holder in 2-digit numbers
- know the difference between the number names, e.g. thirty and thirteen

Concepts covered next year include

- extending place value beyond 3 digits
- reading, writing and ordering numbers to 10 000
- recognising and using the signs for greater than and less than

Assessment points

- ordering whole numbers to 1000
- identifying the value of digits within numbers to 1000
- reading numbers correctly

Chief misconceptions

- reversing digits through a lack of understanding that the position of a digit contributes to its value
- reversing digits through reading numbers backwards rather than from a lack of understanding of place value
- lack of understanding of how numbers are composed of digits, e.g. writing 1006 for 106
- failing to use the appropriate number name depending on the position of the digit, e.g. referring to the 6 digit in 162 as '6' rather than as '60'
- reading scales from the next mark rather than from the one just passed
- not appreciating that the intervals on a scale can change

Place value 1.1 Introducing hundreds

Objectives
- read and write whole numbers to at least 500 in figures and words
- know what each digit represents
- partition a number into a multiple of 10 and ones (TU), or a multiple of 100, a multiple of 10 and ones (HTU)

Key idea	The position of a digit tells us its value.

Teaching model

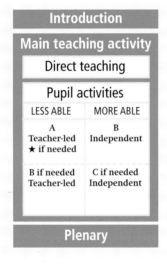

Introduction
Main teaching activity
Direct teaching
Pupil activities

LESS ABLE	MORE ABLE
A Teacher-led ★ if needed	B Independent
B if needed Teacher-led	C if needed Independent

Plenary

Key words   units or ones, tens, hundreds, digit, 1-, 2-, 3-digit number, place value

You need   IP 4   21–22   CM 15

12 cards showing these numbers in figures and words: 52, 174, 206, 260, 379, 471
lists of words for all the units, tens and hundreds numbers to help with spelling
place value cards for all children
several £1, 10p, 1p coins

Introduction: oral work and mental calculation

about 10 minutes
1. Count on in 10s from any small number till you pass 100, then back again. Repeat several times.
2. Choose a child to write a 2-digit number on the board. In unison, the class reads the number aloud and then says the number which is 10 less, then 10 more. Repeat.
3. Play 'Guess my number': Choose a child to write a 2-digit number on a piece of paper. Through 'yes'/'no' responses to questions children establish the decade, whether the number is odd or even, and finally the units digit.

Main teaching input and pupil activities

Direct teaching

about 20 minutes
Use IP 4. On 6 runners, write the same identification numbers as on the prepared cards.
1. Hold up card 52. *Who can point to the runner wearing this number?* Ask a child to read the number, find the card with 52 written in

words and hold it up. Point out the hyphen between fifty and two (included in numbers 21–99).
2. Hold up card 379, covering the 3 with your hand. Ask the class to read the 2-digit then the 3-digit number. Choose a child to point to that runner on the track and to find the 'number in words' card.
What does the digit 3 in 379 represent? And the 7? and the 9? Establish that 379 is equivalent to 3 hundreds, 7 tens and 9 units.

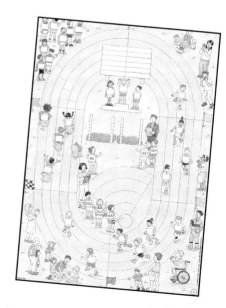

3. Continue to read the remaining cards in figures and words, matching numbers to runners as above.

4. Give the number cards to 6 children. Ask them to form a line in order from 52 to 471. Discuss the cards 206 and 260. Repeat for 174 and 471.

5. Using place value cards, children make 174. Talk about 174 as 100 + 70 + 4. Repeat for the remaining cards.

6. *At Sports Day, we collected 286p in pennies at the gate. We want to change this for £1, 10p and 1p coins. How many of each will we have?*
   Copy this diagram on to the board and discuss the £.p notation.

pennies	£1	10p	1p	total
286p	2	8	6	£2.86

Repeat several times with other numbers of pennies.

Pupil activities

about 15 minutes

LESS ABLE   Teacher-led

CORE A CM 15

Ask all children to make three 3-digit numbers with their place value cards, and write them in figures and in words. Introduce CM 15. Use coins for question 2 if appropriate.

SUPPORT ★

Children practise forming and reading further 3-digit numbers with place value cards.

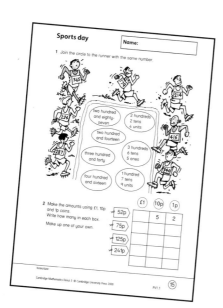

MORE ABLE   Independent

CORE B TB pages 21–22 IP 4

EXTENSION C TB page 22

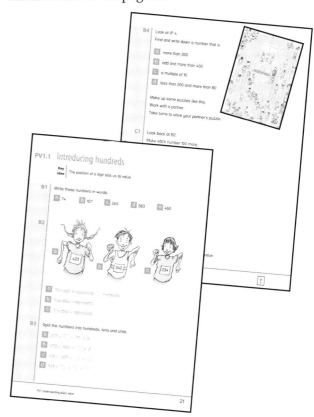

Optional adult input to groups

More able: Help children with the restrictions in question B4 if needed.

Plenary

about 10 minutes

Key idea	The position of a digit tells us its value.

1. Write a 3-digit number in words on the board. Invite a child to come up and write it in numerals. Repeat with other numbers.

2. On IP 4 write some numbers between 100 and 500 on the runners' vests, e.g. 438. Choose children to read the numbers in 2 ways: four hundred and thirty-eight and four hundreds, three tens and eight ones.

Homework suggestion

Children choose six 3-digit race numbers and write them in extended notation. Some children may find it helpful to use place value cards for this task.

Place value 1.2 Changing hundreds

Objectives
- investigate number patterns made by successively adding or subtracting 1, 10 or 100 to numbers up to 500 in a variety of contexts
- say the number that is 1, 10 or 100 more than any given number
- recognise simple patterns and relationships, generalise and predict
- suggest extensions – ask 'What if...?' or 'What could I try next?'

Key idea | When we count on or back in 100s, the digits in the tens and units positions stay the same.

Teaching model

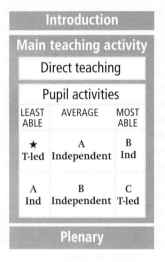

Introduction		
Main teaching activity		
Direct teaching		
Pupil activities		
LEAST ABLE	AVERAGE	MOST ABLE
★ T-led	A Independent	B Ind
A Ind	B Independent	C T-led
Plenary		

Key words units or ones, tens, hundreds, digit, place value

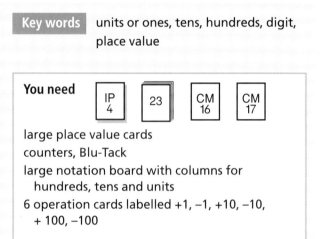

You need | IP 4 | 23 | CM 16 | CM 17

large place value cards
counters, Blu-Tack
large notation board with columns for hundreds, tens and units
6 operation cards labelled +1, −1, +10, −10, + 100, −100

Introduction: oral work and mental calculation

about 10 minutes

1. Play 'Pass the paper':
   Ask one child in each group to write a 3-digit number on a scrap of paper, fold the paper and pass it to another child in the group. This child secretly unfolds the paper and whispers the number to a neighbour. The neighbour now writes the number on a large piece of paper, looking to its originator to confirm the match. Repeat several times. Increase the number of children involved in passing on the whispered number.

Main teaching input and pupil activities

Direct teaching

about 15 minutes

1. On IP 4, point to the podium for the 3 prize winners.
   Imagine the number 381 on the vest of the winner.

Which is the tens digit? The hundreds digit? The units digit?
Swap the units and hundreds digits round and you will have the number of the person who came second. What number is it?
The third winner wore the same 3 digits, with 8 in the units position. What could this number be?

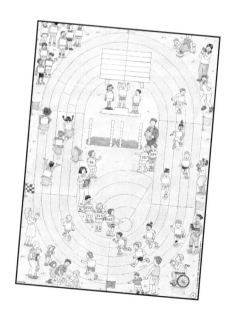

2. Write six 3-digit numbers on the results board. Include a 9 in the units position.
Taking each 3-digit number in turn, ask individual children to say the number that is 1 more /1 less. Model with place value cards. *Which digits change? Which digits stay the same?* Repeat for numbers that are 10 more/less and 100 more/less.

3. Show the notation board. Take 6 counters and stick them randomly with Blu-Tack to the board, putting some in each section, say 2, 3 and 1. Ask the children to say how many counters are in each section, beginning with the hundreds: 2 hundreds, 3 tens, 1 unit. *What number is that? Yes, 231.*

4. Blu-Tack four more counters. Choose a child to place a counter in any of the three sections. Ask how much was added, 1, 10 or 100, and what number is now represented. Repeat 3 more times.
If time permits, extend the activity to taking away counters one at a time from any section, identifying the value of the counter removed.

Pupil activities

about 20 minutes

CORE   Independent

A and B   CM 16

SUPPORT ★ Teacher-led

Shuffle the 6 operation cards. Use IP 4 with the numbers you wrote in the results board. In turn, children take the top card and add or subtract as indicated from a given number in the picture.

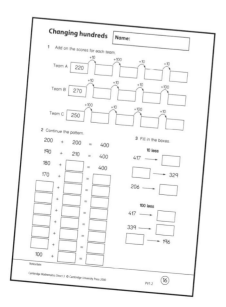

EXTENSION C Independent TB page 23 CM 17
Encourage a systematic recording of the numbers generated by 10 counters.

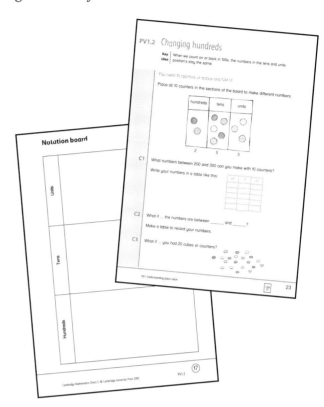

Optional adult input to groups
Core: Help children to focus on which digits are changing and which are staying the same.

Plenary

about 10 minutes

Key idea	When we count on or back in 100s, the digits in the tens and units positions stay the same.

1. Look at CM 16. Elicit the final scores for each team in question 1, and the winning team.
2. Look at CM 16. Ask children to continue the sequence started in 2. Start with 100 and 300.
3. Use the operation cards for a counting activity. Begin at 50, count on in ones. After a few numbers clap to signal a change. Hold up another card, e.g. +10. Continue to redirect the counting, holding up different cards.

Homework suggestion
Children can write a sequence adding 10 to 100, 200, 300, 400, 500 etc.

Place value 1.3 Comparing numbers

Objectives
- compare and order a set of familiar numbers
- use, read and begin to write ordinal numbers and abbreviations, and associated vocabulary

Key idea	We can put things in order and describe their postion with special words.

Teaching model

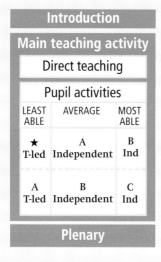

Introduction		
Main teaching activity		
Direct teaching		
Pupil activities		
LEAST ABLE	AVERAGE	MOST ABLE
★ T-led	A Independent	B Ind
A T-led	B Independent	C Ind
Plenary		

Key words order, position, first, second, third, fourth, ..., smallest, largest, between

You need   IP 4   24–25 CM 18

6 operation cards: +1, −1, +10, −10, +100, −100
cards showing 98, 267, 283, 295, 329
counters, Blu-Tack, large blank 100 square or enlarged version of CM 54
red and yellow washable spirit pens

Introduction: oral work and mental calculation

about 10 minutes

1. Play 'Change':
a Write these operations on the board or use the cards from Place value 1.2: +1, −1, +10, −10, +100, −100.
b Begin counting around the class in 1s or 10s from any 2-digit number. After about 4 or 5 numbers, clap and point to a new operation to change the count. Continue counting on and back in multiples of 1, 10 and 100, between 0 and 500.
2. Adapt 'Elimination' (page 32) or 'Guess my number' (page 54) to include 3-digit numbers.

Main teaching input and pupil activities

Direct teaching

about 15 minutes

1. Use IP 4. Divide the class into the red and yellow teams. Randomly allocate runners in the race to each team. Ask children to write in identification letters and to colour vests.
Which runner is in the lead? Which team? What's the letter?
Which runner is second? Third? Last?
2. Write in a column: first, second, third, fourth, ... tenth; and opposite each ordinal word elicit and write the vest letter of the runner. Introduce the abbreviations by underlining the last two letters of each ordinal word: fir<u>st</u>, 1st; seco<u>nd</u>, 2nd; ...

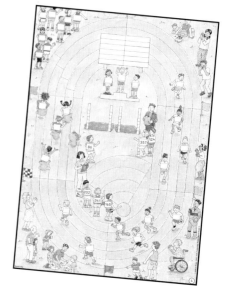

3. Indicate the flags on the track. Discuss the race positions of the runners.
   How many runners are between the orange and purple flags?
   In which section is the 3rd runner? The 2nd team B runner? The fourth team A runner?
4. Have a look at the results of the javelin throwers. Write these distances on the results board on IP 4: A 295 cm, B 267 cm, C 329 cm, D 98 cm, E 283 cm.
   It's quite hard to see who is the winner. How can we arrange these numbers to make it easier? Ask a child to try and put the cards showing the distances, in order. Elicit the best ways of doing this. (compare cards by hundreds first, then tens, ...)
   Who was first, last, third, fifth, ...?
5. Use a large blank 100 square and 8 counters with Blu-Tack. *Now we're going to look at some much higher 'position names'.*
   Write these numbers on the board: 5, 11, 17, 31, 48, 52, 66, 83. Choose a child and say: *Put your counter on the fifth square.* Continue until all the counters are placed.
   Repeat the activity with different numbers. Choose children to make the ordinal statements and to locate the position of the counters on the 100 square.

Pupil activities

about 20 minutes

CORE   Independent   TB pages 24–25
A and B Some children may find it helpful to write the 8 numbers on pieces of paper which

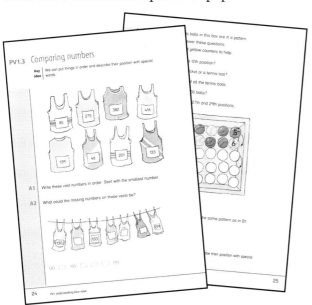

they can order before writing their answers to A1. Have a supply of yellow and red counters available for those children who need help in seeing the pattern is B1.

SUPPORT ★ Teacher-led   CM 18

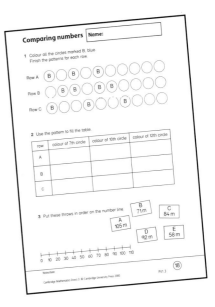

EXTENSION C Independent   TB page 25
Children can use counters to find the position of all the tennis balls.

Optional adult input to groups
Core: Help children to use counters if necessary and practise using correct vocabulary.

Plenary

about 10 minutes

Key idea	We can put things in order and describe their postion with special words.

1. Briefly review the textbook and copymaster tasks.
2. On the board write, say: R Y Y R Y R R Y Y R
   This is the order in which the teams finished the race. In which position is the second/fourth team R/Y runner?
   Which team had a runner in third/sixth position?

Homework suggestion
Ask children to find examples of ordinal numbers, e.g. position of teams in football league, the order that numbers appear in the lottery, street names.

Place value 2.1 Investigating 3-digit numbers

Objectives • read and write whole numbers to at least 1000 in figures and words
• recognise 0 as a place holder in 3-digit numbers
• investigate and compare the largest/smallest numbers that can be made with 3 digits

Key idea	The value of a digit depends on its position.

Teaching model

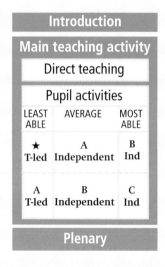

Key words units or ones, tens, hundreds, numeral, digit, 3-digit number, place value, zero, largest, smallest, odd, even

You need

abacus, large number cards 0–9, place value cards for all children, dice dotted 1–6

Introduction: oral work and mental calculation

about 5 minutes

Say 637. Children then make it with their place value cards. Repeat for other numbers.
Say a number and children write it in words.

Main teaching input and pupil activities

Direct teaching

about 15 minutes

1. Display the number 806 on an abacus. *How many beads are on the hundreds wire? The tens wire? The units wire? What number is 8 hundreds and 6 units?*
   Repeat for 860 and discuss the values represented by the beads.

2. On the board make a sketch drawing of abacuses showing 806 and 860. Now rub out the posts and HTU labels. Discuss the uncertainty posed by the removal of the framework and the need to include a 0 as a place holder to show the true position and real value of the digits.

3. Say another number that has 0 as a place holder, e.g. 740. In pairs, one child writes the number in figures and the other writes it in words. They swap to check their work.

4. Lay a set of place value cards face down on the table. Divide the class into 3 groups and invite 3 children from each group to take a card from each pile so that between them they have a hundreds card, a tens card and a units card. Ask each trio to stand in line to display the number that they make with their 3 cards.
   Which group has the largest number? The second largest? When you compare two 3-digit numbers, what do you look for first?
   Look at this number. What if the hundreds digit and the tens digit were swapped, what number would we have then? Repeat for the other numbers.

5. *Which group has the smallest number? The second smallest? How do you know?*
   What is the value of the 6, the 3, the 9?

6. Ask a child to pick 3 digit cards.
   Make the smallest number you can. Now make the largest. When you are making the smallest/largest number possible with your 3 cards, what is the best place to put the largest digit? The smallest digit?

7. Repeat the activity several times to give all children a turn.

Pupil activities

about 20 minutes

CORE   Independent

A TB page 26
Children could use the number cards 0–9 to help them realise that the tens digit stays the same whilst the units and hundreds digits interchange.

B TB page 27
Children generate 3-digit numbers with 0 in the tens or units place and order a set of such numbers.

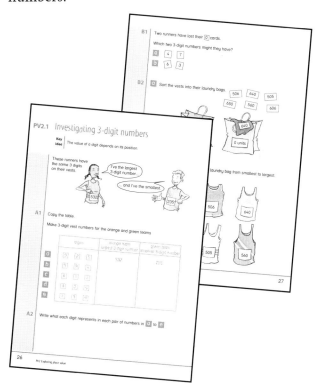

SUPPORT ★ Teacher-led
Give each pair a dice and the place value cards: 500–900, 10–60 and 1–6. Children take turns to select a 3-digit number card (e.g. 700) and roll the dice (e.g. 4). They then choose whether to make the 4 represent 4 tens or 4 units and select the corresponding place value card to form the 3-digit number (740 or 704) for their partner to read aloud.

EXTENSION C Independent TB page 28
Children investigate the different 3-digit numbers that can be formed by using 3 digits.

Optional adult input to groups
Core and extension: Remind children that the hundreds digit is the most significant in determining how large a number is.

Plenary

about 10 minutes

Key idea	The value of a digit depends on its position.

1. Write on the board the pairs of numbers generated in question A1.
   What do you notice about each pair of numbers? Which digit stays in place? Which digits swap over? Which team has the largest/smallest number? Read the number out loud.
   Which number is nearest to 600?
2. On the board write 89. Beside it write 089, 0089, 00089. Discuss the redundancy of the zeros in that they are not acting as place holders and the value of the number is unchanged whatever the number of zeros to the left.
   The number may look larger and longer but it is still 89.

Homework suggestion
Find 5 examples of numbers round the home with zero as a place holder, e.g. Teletext and Ceefax numbers, weights and measures.

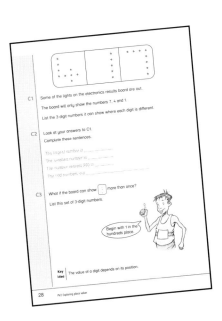

Place value 2.2 Adding and subtracting 1, 10 or 100

Objectives
- investigate number patterns made by adding or subtracting successively 1, 10 or 100 to numbers up to 1000
- use and apply findings in a number of contexts: find missing numbers in partial hundred squares, use measures and money
- recognise simple patterns or relationships, generalise and predict

Key idea | If you add or subtract 10 or 100, the units digit stays the same.

Teaching model

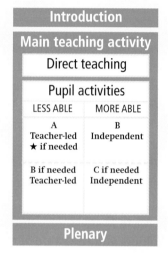

Key words units, tens, hundreds, digit, 3-digit number, place value, more, less, least, smallest, largest, greatest

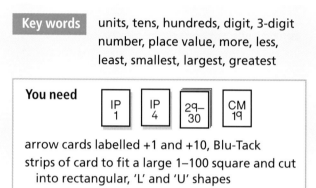

You need

arrow cards labelled +1 and +10, Blu-Tack
strips of card to fit a large 1–100 square and cut into rectangular, 'L' and 'U' shapes
1–100 squares (CM 52), interlocking cubes

Introduction: oral work and mental calculation

about 5 minutes

1. Play 'Zero in':
   - *My number is less than 600 and more than 200.*
   - *It has 6 units.*
   - *It has zero in the tens place.*
   What might my number be? (506, 406 or 306)

2. Write a 3-digit number on a runner's vest on IP 4. Begin counting around the class in 1s. After about 10 numbers, change the count by clapping and saying '2s/10s'. For example: ..., 358, 359, 360, (clap, +2) 362, 364, ..., 376, 378, (clap, +10) 388, 398, ...
   Repeat for different numbers. Include counting back in 1s, 2s or 10s.

Main teaching input and pupil activities

Direct teaching

about 15 minutes

1. Point to 12 on the 1–100 square and ask the class to count along the row to 19. *By how much do the numbers increase each time?* Blu-Tack the +1 card to the top of the grid.
   Now ask the class to say the numbers in the column, beginning at 12. Establish an increase of ten and Blu-Tack the +10 card to the left side of the grid. Repeat for other starting numbers.

2. *What's 12, add 1, then add 10? What number do you have? Now add 1, then 10 to 23. What's your answer?* Continue in this way to 56. Discuss the diagonal pattern, inviting quick ways to continue it (add on 11). Repeat, beginning at 25.

3. *What if we had a 101 to 200 square and we add 1 plus 10 to any number, will the answer be on the diagonal line?* Investigate.

4. Place a rectangular strip of card over a column or row and ask children to name the hidden numbers. Repeat with 'L' and 'U' shape cards. Discuss the rules for finding the missing numbers. (row, add 1; column, add 10; diagonal, add 11)

5. Write the number 756 on the board. *What number is 1 more/less than 756? 10 more/less than 756? 100 more/less than 756?*

   Build up the table:

755	756	757
746	756	766
656	756	856

   Encourage a search for patterns in each row and column. *What's changing? What's staying the same?*

   Repeat, starting with a measure or money.

6. Refer to IP 4. *There was a difference of 10p in each of the 3 amounts collected in entry fees for 3 races. If the greatest/middle/least amount was £7.60, what are the other amounts?*

Pupil activities

about 20 minutes
LESS ABLE   Teacher-led
CORE A CM 19
Children find the missing numbers in complete and partial 1–100 squares.

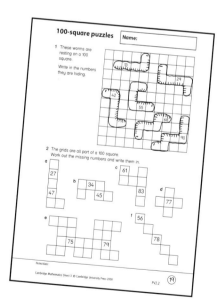

SUPPORT ★
Provide each pair with an A4 100 square and 5 interlocking cubes. Children take it in turns to make 'L', 'U' or '+' shapes with the 5 cubes which they place on the 1–100 square. Their partner has to identify the numbers covered by the cubes.

MORE ABLE   Independent TB pages 29–30
CORE B Children look at sequences that are generated by adding or subtracting successively 1, 10 or 100 to/from numbers up to 1000.
EXTENSION C
Children add or subtract 1, 10 or 100 to/from a sum of money. They look for a quick way to find the difference between the least and greatest amounts.

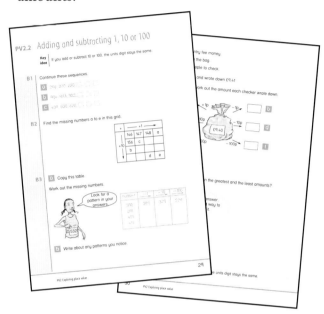

Optional adult input to groups
More able: Help children to imagine the 1–100 square in their minds and to use the patterns to help them rather than counting on or back.

Plenary

about 10 minutes

Key idea	If you add or subtract 10 or 100, the units digit stays the same.

1. Ask a child to state their answers to question 2f of CM 19. Discuss the pattern generated by adding 11: 56, 67, 78, 89, 100. *Why is the last number 100 and not 90?*

2. Review the answers to TB question B2. *What if the given numbers were 246, 247, 248 and 256? What effect would this have on your answers a to e?*

Homework suggestion
Children select three 3-digit numbers. They find the numbers that are 1, 10 and 100 more and less than their chosen number.

Place value 2.3 Numbers between

Objectives	• compare two numbers
	• find a page between two others
	• state the number half way between two numbers in the contexts of measurement and money
	• name the odd and even numbers lying between two numbers

Key idea	We can compare two numbers and find a number between them.

Teaching model

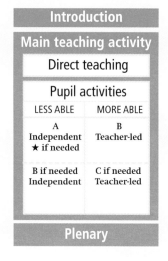

Introduction

Main teaching activity

Direct teaching

Pupil activities	
LESS ABLE	MORE ABLE
A Independent ★ if needed	B Teacher-led
B if needed Independent	C if needed Teacher-led

Plenary

Key words units, tens, hundreds , digit, 3-digit number, place value, more, less, fewer, between, half way, difference between, odd, even

You need

IP 4   31   CM 20

cards labelled, 'U', 'T' and 'H', base 10 materials, HTU boards, cubes, counting stick, book, purse

Introduction: oral work and mental calculation

about 5 minutes

Play 'Place invaders':

Write a 3-digit number on the board, e.g. 529. Give the cards labelled 'U', 'T' and 'H' to 3 children. The child with the U card begins, saying, '529, zapp the 9 leaves 520.' The child with T says, '520, zapp the 20 leaves 500.' The child with H says: 500, zapp the 500 leaves 0.' Repeat with other 3-digit numbers.

Main teaching input and pupil activities

Direct teaching

about 15 minutes

1. Look at IP 4. Label the orange flag 500 m and the blue flag 600 m. Discuss and compare the estimated positions of the runners between the flags. *Which runner is nearest to the 600 m mark? The 500 m mark? About how many metres do you think the leading runner has run?* (e.g. 580 m).

The last runner? (e.g. 530 m) Colour both vests, one red, one blue to assist identification. *Which is more/less, 580 or 530?*
Repeat the activity for other pairs of runners.

2. Ask a child to estimate a point half way between the 500 m and the 600 m flags, and colour the vest of the nearest runner, green.

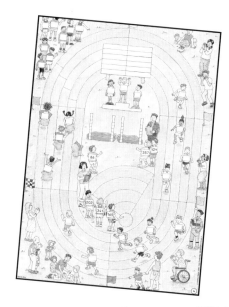

If the green-vested runner was exactly half way between 500 m and 600 m what is the distance in metres? Show with base 10 materials that the difference between 500 and 600 is 100. Demonstrate halving the 100 by exchanging a 100-flat for ten 10-rods which are then halved to make two sets of five 10-rods. Show 500, 550 and 600 in base 10 materials.

3. Hold up a counting stick. Point to the half way position. *The ends are 0 and 10. What number is half way between 10 and 0? Tell me which number is half way when the ends are 0 and 20 / 0 and 100 / 0 and 1000. What if the ends were 50 and 70? Or 500 and 700?* Invite explanations from the children. Focus on halving the difference between the end numbers and then adding the result to the lesser number.

4. Hold up a paperback book. *I'm reading chapter 3 of this book. Chapter 3 runs from page 17 to page 27. What page might I be reading? Name the even/odd numbers between 17 and 27. If the digits of the odd numbered page total 10, which page am I reading?* Repeat for other pairs of numbers.

5. Finish with quickfire questions such as:
I have between £6 and £7 in my purse. How much money might I have?
That box weighs between 12 kg and 17 kg. What weight could it be?
The distance between the classroom and the school gates is between 90 m and 110 m. How far could it be?

Pupil activities

about 20 minutes
LESS ABLE Independent
CORE A   CM 20
The marked intervals on the number lines will help children to find the missing numbers.
SUPPORT ★ TB page 31
Children can use base 10 materials and notation boards to model and compare the pairs of 3-digit numbers.

MORE ABLE Teacher-led
CORE B TB page 31
Children find the numbers between in the contexts of money and measurement.
EXTENSION C
Ask children to make up 3 problems for a friend to solve.

Optional adult input to groups
Core A: Check that children are using the first digits in the numbers to gain a feel for what the number between might be.
Support: Help children to see that measures and money can be expressed as 3-digit numbers too.

Plenary

about 10 minutes

Key idea	We can compare two numbers and find a number between them.

1. Review the work on CM 20.
2. Discuss the range of possible answers to TB questions B1, B2.
3. Extend the textbook questions, for example:
What are the even/odd numbers between 70 and 80?
If you add the digits of Kenny's throw, the answer is 12. How far did he throw the javelin?
Gina's prize cost half way between £8 and £9/ £8.50 and £8.60... cost 1p short of £9/£8.50.

Homework suggestion
Children find 3 examples of estimates as 'numbers between' e.g.
I think that there are between ☐ and ☐ slices in a loaf.
I think that there are between ☐ and ☐ pasta shapes/cornflakes in a serving.
I think that there are between ☐ and ☐ glasses in a bottle of lemonade.

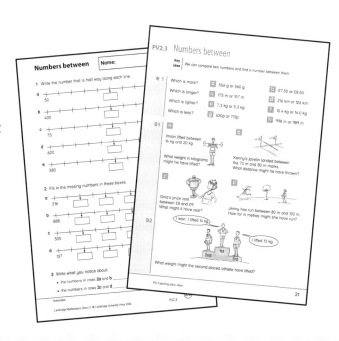

Place value 3.1 Ordering whole numbers

Objectives
- read, write and order whole numbers to at least 1000
- know what each digit represents and partition as 749 = 700 + 40 + 9

Key idea	When we order 3-digit numbers we look first at the hundreds digit, then at the tens digit and finally at the units digit.

Teaching model

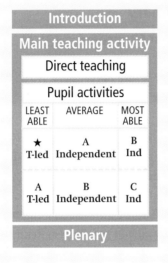

Introduction

Main teaching activity

Direct teaching

Pupil activities

LEAST ABLE	AVERAGE	MOST ABLE
★ T-led	A Independent	B Ind
A T-led	B Independent	C Ind

Plenary

Key words 1-, 2- or 3-digit number, order, before, after, next, between, more/ less/greater/smaller than, equal to

You need

IP 1   IP 5   32–33   CM 21

place value cards for all children
cards numbered 362, 406, 584, 618, 725, 739
Blu-Tack

Introduction: oral work and mental calculation

about 5 minutes

1. Count forward and back again to 0, in 10s to 100 and in 100s to 1000.
2. Ask children to use their place value cards.
   Give me a number that:
   is an even (odd) number greater (less) than 50,
   is a 2-digit number with both digits even (odd),
   is a 2-digit number whose digits add up to 9 (11, 12),
   is a 2-digit number where the tens digit is double (half) the units digit ...
   Locate all the possible answers to the last 2 questions on IP 1.

Main teaching input and pupil activities

Direct teaching

about 15 minutes

1. Use IP 5. Write these numbers on the labels of the bottles on the shelves at the top:
   top shelf   362   739   406   618   725   584
   lower shelf   250   500   750
   Write these numbers in the 3 'explosion

clouds' from the flask on the bench: 700, 40, 9
2. Focus on the array of bottles on the top shelf which are out of reach of the Professor.
   How much liquid is in each bottle?
3. The Professor has a plan. She will put all her bottles and flasks in order on the lower shelf.
4. Elicit the positions of the 250, 500 and 750 flasks in terms of place value.
5. *Where will the Professor put the 362 bottle?*
   Yes, after the 250 flask ... / between the 250 and 500 flasks because 300 is more than 200 and is less than 500 ... Fix the card numbered 362 in place on the lower shelf.

6. Continue to order the remaining bottles on the shelf. Encourage children to use the positional terms, 'before', 'after', 'between', 'next to' and to refer, where appropriate, to the value of the digit in the hundreds and/or tens positions.

7. *While the Mad Professor was ordering her shelf she forgot about her experiment. The flask has exploded into 40 and 9 and 700. What was the number on the flask before the accident?*
    Ask children to use 1-, 2- and 3-digit cards to assemble 749. Write on the board:
    749 = 700 + 40 + 9.

8. Repeat by 'exploding' other 3-digit numbers. Write the numbers and the extended notation on the board using the = sign to represent equality.

Pupil activities

about 20 minutes
CORE Independent
A TB page 32
Children may find it helpful to use their place value cards to model the numbers as extended notation.
B TB page 33

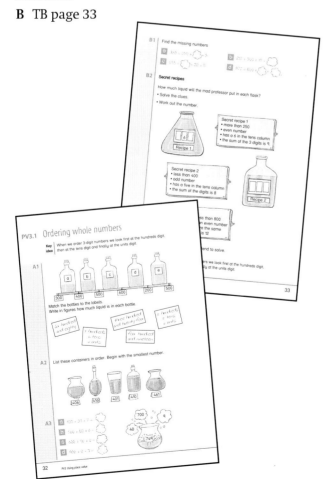

SUPPORT ★ Teacher-led CM 21
Ask questions to help children compare and order the numbers as they join up the dots. Continue supporting children with the core activity.

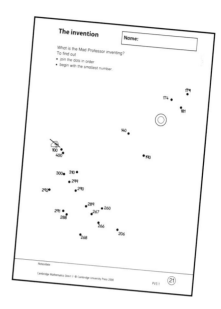

EXTENSION C Independent   TB page 33

Optional adult input to groups
Check that children are looking at the hundreds digit first.

Plenary

about 10 minutes

Key idea	When we order 3-digit numbers we look first at the hundreds digit, then at the tens digit and finally at the units digit.

1. Read each label from A1 in two ways: in words, and in hundreds, tens and units.
2. Pick two of B1 and ask:
    How did you work out the missing numbers?
3. Ask children who tried solving the secret recipes to demonstrate their reasoning.
    Has anyone got another way?
4. Try out one of the invented secret recipes.

Place value 3.2 Comparing

Objectives
- order and compare a set of familiar numbers or measures
- state a number lying between two numbers (up to 3 digits)

Key idea	A number lying between two numbers is greater than the first number and smaller than the second.

Teaching model

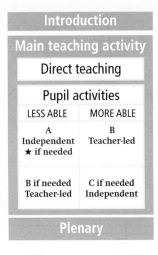

Key words order, last, as many as, equal to, more/less/fewer than, larger, smaller, largest, smallest, next, after, before, between

You need

cards showing 156, 202, 220, 342, 500, 651
cards showing 250 g, 340 g, 430 g, 500 g, 510 g, 1 kg
cards showing 39p, 45p, 66p, 72p, 99p
washing line for hanging cards or Blu-Tack
a large 1–100 number line (CMs 56 and 57), number cards, counters

Introduction: oral work and mental calculation

about 5 minutes

1. *Start at 80. Count on in 1s to 110 and back again to 80.*
   Start at 80. Count on in 10s until you pass 200.
   Start at 80. Count on in 100s to 980.
2. Write numbers on the board.
   Let's read these numbers: 863   680   308
   What is the value of the 8 in 863? in 680? in 308?
3. Repeat for 3, 6 and 0.
4. Repeat for a number such as 686.

Main teaching input and pupil activities

Direct teaching

about 10 minutes

1. *We are going to practise putting numbers in order, and then make some comparisons between them.*
2. Show the class the set of cards with numbers on them. Ask for help in sorting them into order. Hang the cards on a washing line or stick them on the board with Blu-Tack. Give

instructions such as: *Put the smallest/largest number here, then arrange the rest in order.*
3. When the cards are in order ask questions: *What number could go in between the 3rd and 4th numbers? Which number comes after/ before/between ...?*
4. Display the set of cards with measures on them. Tell children to talk to a partner about which is heaviest/lightest/more than half a kilogram ... Draw the class together again, talk through the responses and order the cards on the washing line or board.
   A book weighs more than the weight on the first card, but less than the weight on the second card. What could it weigh? ...

Pupil activities

about 25 minutes
LESS ABLE Independent CM 22
CORE A
Children order and compare 3-digit numbers.
SUPPORT ★
Children can write the numbers on cards and use a number line to order them.

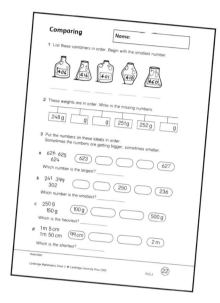

CORE B Teacher-led TB pages 34–35
Place the 'money' cards so that they can all be seen. Pick up '66p'. Ask a child to choose a greater amount, then another child to choose a lesser amount. Point out that your amount is in between and is greater than the smaller amount and smaller than the larger amount.
Ask children to suggest an amount other than this that would be greater than the smaller amount and smaller than the larger amount. Ask children to position the amounts on the number line and ask comparative questions. Introduce the textbook pages.

MORE ABLE
CORE B Teacher-led TB pages 34–35
Introduce as above.
EXTENSION C Independent
Ask children to play 'Compare' using 5 cards, making 4-digit numbers and setting their own target numbers.

Optional adult input to groups
Support: Help children to order cards and ask comparative questions.
Core: Discuss their work with children using the correct vocabulary.
Extension: Encourage children to extend the game by adding their own rules.

Plenary

about 5 minutes

Key idea	A number lying between two numbers is greater than the first number and smaller than the second.

1. Play 'Compare' as a class.
2. Ask some children to talk about the strategies and extra rules they used.
3. Demonstrate the key idea with 5 new numbers.

Homework suggestion
In a purse there are only 3 coins. The coins may be £1, 50p or 20p. Write 5 total amounts that there could be. Put the amounts in order, beginning with the largest.

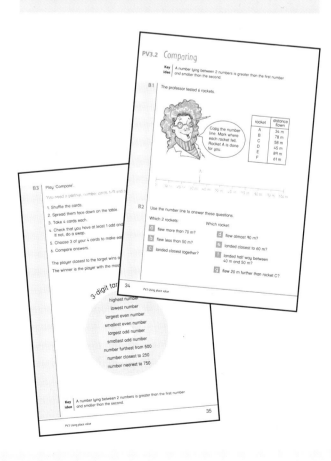

Place value 3.3 Reading scales

Objective • read a scale to the nearest marked division

Key idea	The marked divisions help us to read amounts on a scale.

Teaching model

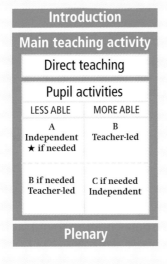

Introduction	
Main teaching activity	
Direct teaching	
Pupil activities	
LESS ABLE	MORE ABLE
A Independent ★ if needed	B Teacher-led
B if needed Teacher-led	C if needed Independent
Plenary	

Key words measuring scale, division, difference

You need

IP 5   36–37   CM 23   CM 24

place value cards for all children
blue washable spirit pens
a current newspaper with weather reports

Introduction: oral work and mental calculation

about 5 minutes

1. Count in 5s to 100 and back again.
   Start from 1 and from 4 (near multiples of 5).
2. Ask children to use their place value cards.
   Give me a number between 10 and 20, 34 and 36, 50 and 100, 55 and 70, 120 and 140.
   Give me an odd/even number between 37 and 40, 60 and 170, 300 and 320.
   Give me a 3-digit number between 95 and 102, ...
   Something weighs more than 200 g and less than 300 g. What could it weigh?
   John is taller than 1m 30 cm and smaller than 1m 40 cm. How tall could he be?

Main teaching input and pupil activities

Direct teaching

about 15 minutes

1. Show children IP 5. Point to the 2 bottles on the bench. The first bottle is marked in intervals of 10. Colour in to the 30 mark.
   How much liquid is in this bottle? Raise the liquid level to about 49 and then to about 85. Ask children to state the measures to the nearest marked interval such as *nearly 50, less than 50*

and *about half way between 80 and 90, about 85.*
2. The second bottle is marked in intervals of 5. Colour in amounts that are multiples of 5, until the bottle is nearly full. Ask children to state the measures for each amount.
3. Discuss and draw a suitable scale for the flask. Ask pupils, in turn, to colour in an amount and invite the class to make appropriate measurement statements.
4. Indicate the 2 beakers with thermometers in. Using these and the large thermometers establish that the scale is marked in intervals of 10 from 0 to 100 and that each interval is further divided to show the units. Compare the marked divisions to

those shown on a ruler. Talk about the temperature when water freezes (at 0°C) and boils (at 100°C).

5. Colour one thermometer in blue to 40°C and the other to 90°C.
   Which beaker of liquid is the warmer? What is the difference in temperature between the two beakers? Repeat with further examples. You may wish to include temperatures that are multiples of 5.

6. Invite pairs of children to choose and colour a temperature reading each. Compare the temperatures.

7. Use some of the other scales on IP 5 to discuss making approximate readings.

Pupil activities

about 25 minutes

LESS ABLE

CORE A   Independent   CM 23

CM 24 may be prepared for further differentiated practice.

CORE B   Teacher-led   TB pages 36–37

SUPPORT ★ Independent

Children can use a prepared copy of CM 24 or IP 5 to practise colouring in temperatures.

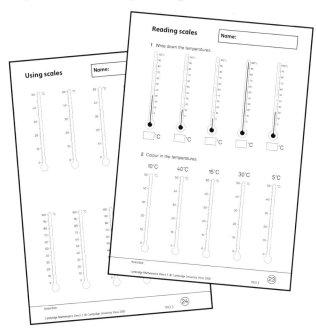

MORE ABLE

CORE B   Teacher-led   TB pages 36–37

EXTENSION C   Independent

Give children a current newspaper that shows temperatures 'Around Britain Yesterday' and 'Abroad'. Ask them to work with a partner to find the warmest and coolest places in Britain and abroad, and to calculate the differences in these temperatures.

Optional adult input to groups

Encourage children to read the numbers on the divisions rather than counting on.

Plenary

about 10 minutes

Key idea	The marked divisions help us to read amounts on a scale.

1. Talk about using complementary addition as a way of checking answers to B2 and B3.

2. Ask children who worked on the extension to talk about their findings.

3. Challenge children to find out what their normal body temperature should be.
   What does it mean when the doctor says, 'Your temperature is up.'?

Homework suggestion

Ask children to use CM 24 to choose and record several temperatures. They could also suggest an appropriate time and place for each temperature – a cold winter's day outside, for example. Encourage them to read any temperature scales they have at home or watch a television weather forecast.

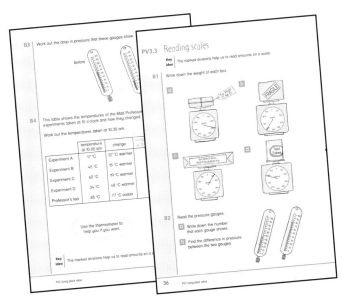

Glossary

Key words and terms to be used with children
sensible, guess how many, estimate, nearest, roughly, about, nearly, approximately, too many, too few, enough, not enough, round up/down, round to the nearest 10/100, position, before, next, after, half way, nearest

estimate   an informed 'guess' based on knowledge and existing evidence

approximately   usually used when describing the magnitude of something as being close to a particular number

General overview of the topic

Estimating quantities is something we do every day when we don't need to know exact amounts but just need to have enough, or when we want a rough idea for making plans. Children need to learn strategies for making sensible estimates. These strategies involve learning from their previous experience as well as from the situation before them.

Being able to estimate the position of a number on a number line means that children have a feel for that number's magnitude and its closeness to multiples of 10 and 100. It's a skill that is useful when ordering and rounding numbers.

We round numbers to the nearest 10 or 100 when doing a rough calculation or again when the exact number or measurement is not needed.

Estimating and rounding
Children practise making sensible estimates and explain their strategies. They also practise rounding numbers to the nearest 10.

Links between blocks

Lessons in this block tie in with lessons in the three place value blocks and each may be taught after or alongside one of those blocks.

Before they start, children need to

- estimate a number up to about 50 and be able to explain their estimate
- identify the position of any number on a 100 square or number line
- begin to round numbers less than 100 to the nearest 10

Concepts covered next year include

- estimating the answers to calculations by rounding
- comparing estimates

Assessment points

- rounding any number less than 100 to the nearest 10 and any 3-digit number to the nearest 100
- positioning any number on a 0–100 number line

Chief misconceptions

- not fully understanding when to round up and when to round down

Rounding 1.1 Collections and numbers

Objectives
- make sensible estimates for numbers and collections in a range of practical contexts to about 100
- explain how estimates are made and justify why they are reasonable
- use the vocabulary of estimation

Key idea	Sometimes we can estimate rather than count exactly.

Teaching model

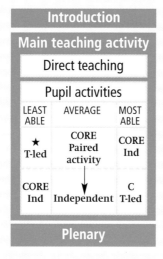

Key words   sensible, guess how many, about, roughly, approximately, too many, too few, enough, not enough, estimate

You need

jar containing enough sweets or grapes for each child to have one

10 transparent containers of varying sizes filled with fewer than 100 small objects, e.g. beads, shells, cubes, sweets

cards showing random arrangements of up to 20 symbols (e.g. spots) and between 20 and 100 symbols

Introduction: oral work and mental calculation

about 5 minutes

Show a card with up to 20 spots on it for a few seconds. Hide the card and ask children to guess how many spots they saw. Count and check. Ask children to explain how they made their guesses. Repeat with other cards.

Main teaching input and pupil activities

Direct teaching

about 15 minutes

1. *Sometimes we do not need to know exactly how many we have of something. We can estimate instead.* Ask children to remind each other of what estimating means.
2. Hold up a container of sweets or grapes. *Have we got enough here for everyone to have one? Roughly how many are there in the jar?*
3. Take a range of estimates from children. Discuss. Do any estimates stand out as impossible, unlikely? Establish a realistic range of possibilities and write this on the board.
4. Ask children to explain how they made their estimates. Discuss strategies. Are some strategies quicker, easier to use than others? Are they sensible?
5. Count how many there are in the jar. *Are there enough?*
6. Remind children that they were not asked to find the exact number but to make a sensible estimate. How close were their estimates? Who was nearest? Did it matter that they did not work out the exact number? Discuss other occasions when it is more important to have enough and roughly the right number rather than the exact amount (biscuits for a tea party, chairs at a party).

Pupil activities

about 20 minutes

CORE   Independent   CM 25

Paired activity

Set out the selection of transparent containers. Label them A, B, C, ...

Tell children that in this activity they have to estimate how many objects there are in each container. Explain how to record their estimates on CM 25. Children work collaboratively in pairs.

SUPPORT ★ Teacher-led   CM 25

Repeat Direct teaching activities 2–5 using a container holding a smaller number of objects. Encourage each child to give an estimate and explain it. Emphasise the sensible nature of estimating. Start the group working on other containers of objects recording their estimates on CM 25, then leave them to finish independently.

EXTENSION C Teacher-led

Children look around the classroom for opportunities to estimate numbers, e.g. the number of children around the room, books, pencils in a tray. Tell children that they are estimating the numbers of both organised collections of things and randomly arranged things. How does this affect their ability to estimate?

Optional adult input to groups

Core: Encourage children to pick up the containers carefully and look closely at the contents.

Plenary

about 10 minutes

Key idea	Sometimes we can estimate rather than count exactly.

1. Look at all the containers. Ask children to give their estimates for each container in turn, then count the objects together so that they can fill in the actual number on CM 25. Ask children to discuss with a partner whether their estimates were sensible and to complete the final column.

2. Ask the rest of the class to tell the extension group what they think they did and ask questions about it. The extension group should also explain why estimating random groups of objects is harder than estimating neatly arranged collections.

3. Ask general questions about estimating:
   When is it difficult to count the exact number?
   When is it unnecessary to know the exact number?
   Why is useful to be able to make an estimate?

Homework suggestion

Choose something at home to estimate how many you have got, e.g. socks, pasta shapes in a packet, nails in a tool box, ... Estimate first, then count exactly. How close was the estimate? Was the estimate sensible?

Rounding 1.2 Number lines

Objectives
- estimate the position of a number on a number line
- explain how estimates are made and justify why they are reasonable
- round numbers to the nearest 10

Key idea	We can estimate the position of numbers on a number line.

Teaching model

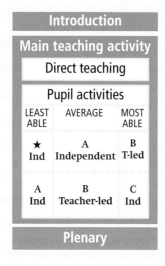

Key words position, before, next, after, half way, nearest

You need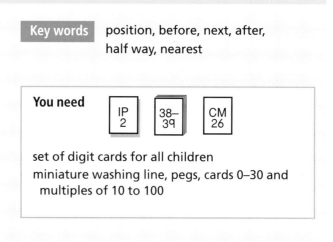

set of digit cards for all children
miniature washing line, pegs, cards 0–30 and multiples of 10 to 100

Introduction: oral work and mental calculation

about 5 minutes

1. Say a number under 20 and ask children to show the number that is half that number. Repeat for other numbers.
2. With children working in pairs, ask for doubles of numbers.

Main teaching input and pupil activities

Direct teaching

about 20 minutes

1. Show children the washing lines on IP 2. *Sometimes it is more useful to use a number line that doesn't have all the numbers on it. This lesson is about how to estimate the position of a number on a number line.*
2. Show children the miniature washing line. Label the left-hand end zero and the right-hand end 10. Ask three children to choose a number between 0 and 10 and to peg each card on the line. Ask each child to explain why they chose the position they did. Once all 3

numbers are on the line ask the class to say whether the numbers are in the right order. Do they need to change anything?
3. Change the range of the washing line, e.g. to 15–25. Repeat activity 2 with other numbers. Include numbers outside the range so that children have the opportunity to notice and tell you that it is not possible to place these numbers on the line.
4. Change the range to 0–100. This time peg on multiples of ten.

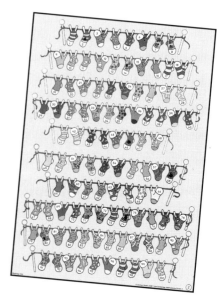

5. Revise the strategies that children have been using and identify the most useful ones.
6. Ask children what multiples of 10 are 'on either side' of various 2-digit numbers.
   How might knowing this help you to position a number on a number line?

Pupil activities

about 20 minutes

CORE

A Independent   TB page 38

B Teacher-led   TB page 39

Children draw the number lines in their books and decide where the numbers should go.

SUPPORT ★ Independent   CM 26

Children practise locating specific points on a 0–20 number line.

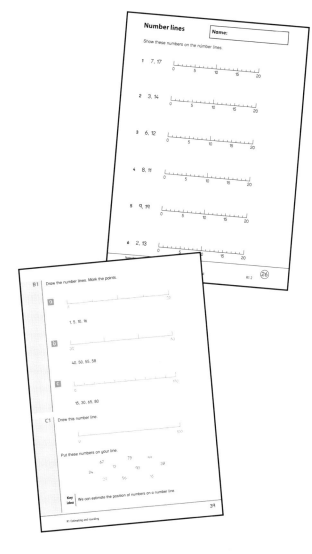

EXTENSION C Independent   TB page 39

Children work out where to position numbers when there are no divisions on a number line.

Optional adult input to groups

Core A: Ask children to compare the numbers and so decide where they should lie on the line.

Support: Check that children are comparing numbers to find the position, rather than just counting the divisions.

Extension: Check that children look at the tens digit as an indicator of where a number might lie on the line.

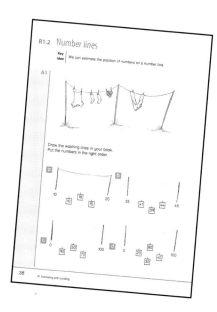

Plenary

about 10 minutes

Key idea	We can estimate the position of numbers on a number line.

1. Look at IP 2. Select lines marked in 50s, 20s and 5s. Cover the other lines. *How do we know what the divisions indicate? How can we use this information to help us estimate the position of a number?*
2. Place the same number, e.g. 25, on each line. Discuss the strategies used to work out where it should go.
3. Make a list of children's strategies on the board. Discuss with children and rearrange in order of usefulness.

Homework suggestion

Put the street numbers of 5 friends and your own on to an empty number line.

Rounding 1.3 Rounding to 10 and 100

Objectives
- round numbers less than 100 to the nearest 10
- begin to approximate by rounding any 3-digit number to the nearest hundred

| Key idea | We can decide whether to round numbers up or down by looking at the units or tens digits. |

Teaching model

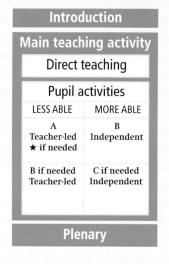

Key words   round up/down, round to the nearest 10/100, nearest, roughly, nearly, approximately

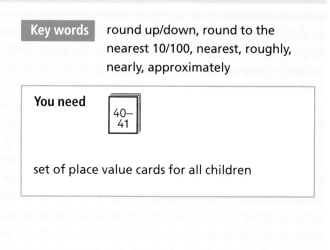

Introduction: oral work and mental calculation

about 5 minutes

1. Count on in 10s from 0 to 100 and back again. Count on in hundreds from 0 to 1000 and back again.
2. Play 'Next 10':
   Call out a 2-digit number and children hold up the next tens number.
   Play 'Last 10':
   Call out a 2-digit number and children hold up the tens number before it.

Main teaching input and pupil activities

Direct teaching

about 15 minutes

1. Remind children of the rules for rounding to the nearest 10, especially that the numbers with units digit of 5 round up.
2. Call out 2-digit numbers for children to round to the nearest 10.
3. Write 20 on the board. *Which numbers round up or down to 20?*

4. Collect and write up children's answers (15, 16, 17, 18, 19, 21, 22, 23, 24). Ask children to explain why they chose to include each number.
5. Look at the numbers. *How many are there?* Sort the numbers by tens digit and then by units digit. *Which digit decides what the nearest 10 is?*
6. Repeat 2–5 with another tens number.
7. *If the rule is that 5 rounds up when rounding to the nearest 10, what do you think the rule will be for rounding to the nearest 100?*
8. Establish that 50+ will round up. *Which digit will we need to look at to decide the nearest 100?* Look at a 3-digit number, e.g. 273. *Which 2 hundreds numbers does 273 lie between? Which is it nearer to?* Look at the tens digit and round up to 300.
   Record on the board: 200   273 → 300
   Repeat for other 3-digit numbers.
9. Write 500 on the board. Collect 3-digit numbers that will round to 500 and write them around it. *What do we notice about these numbers?* Discuss which numbers make up the set, i.e. the numbers between 450 and 549 inclusive.

Pupil activities

about 20 minutes
LESS ABLE   Teacher-led
CORE A TB pages 40-41
Children practise rounding numbers to the nearest 10 or 100.
SUPPORT ★ TB page 40
This provides practice in rounding to 10 or 20.

MORE ABLE   Independent
CORE B TB page 41
Children practise choosing numbers that round to a particular 10 or 100.
EXTENSION C TB page 41
Children choose their own numbers to round to.

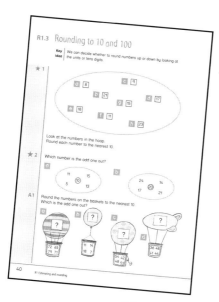

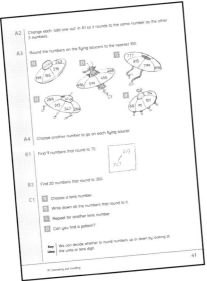

Optional adult input to groups
Check that children are focusing on the appropriate digit when rounding.

Plenary

about 10 minutes

Key idea	We can decide whether to round numbers up or down by looking at the units or tens digits.

1. Play 'Rounding bingo':
   Children sit with partner, less able with more able, and draw a 2 × 2 grid. Children choose 4 tens numbers from 0 to 100 and write them on the grid. Call 2-digit numbers at random, keeping a record of the numbers. Children round each number to the nearest ten and cross it off their grid if they have it. First pair to cross off all their numbers are the winners. During the activity, monitor children's pace and accuracy with rounding.
2. Repeat for hundreds.
3. Invite a child to give a set of numbers that all round to the same tens/hundreds number and ask the rest of the class to work out what the number is that they are rounding to.

Homework suggestion
Design a simple board game (Bingo style or other), colouring sheet (colour by number or other) or puzzle, e.g. dot-to-dot, based on rounding numbers to nearest 10 or 100.

Glossary

Key words and terms to be used with children
part, divided, fraction, one whole, one half, one quarter, one third, one fifth, one tenth, equal, not equal, unequal, same as, half way, two quarters, three quarters, two thirds

fraction   the size of each part when something is divided into equal parts

denominator   shows the number of parts into which the whole has beeen divided

numerator   the number of parts you are interested in

equivalent fractions   fractions that have the same value, e.g. $\frac{1}{2}$ and $\frac{2}{4}$

mixed fraction   a number that is made up of a whole number and a fraction, e.g. $3\frac{1}{2}$

General overview of the topic

The standard notation for fractions can sometimes make this a difficult area for children. They need to understand how the notation works, how to read it and how to write it themselves. Having a good understanding of this will help children to compare fractions successfully as they will appreciate that the greater the denominator then the smaller each part of the whole must be.

Grasping the concept of equivalence makes appreciating the relative magnitude of fractions much easier. Knowing that $\frac{5}{10}$ is equivalent to $\frac{1}{2}$ helps children to see that $\frac{7}{10}$ is greater than $\frac{1}{2}$.

Fractions 1: Simple fractions
Children find unitary fractions of shapes, sets of objects and of numbers. Understanding of the significance of the denominator is developed.

Fractions 2: Extending fractions
The equivalence of fractions is explored and children find simple non-unit fractions of shapes.

Fractions 3: Comparing fractions
Children see fractions as numbers and position them on the number line.

Links between blocks

Fractions 1 extends what children know about halves and quarters to other simple unit fractions. Fractions 2 and 3 then develop these ideas and could be taught in successive terms.

Before they start, children need to

- recognise halves and quarters of shapes and sets
- read the notation for halves and quarters
- appreciate the equivalence between $\frac{2}{4}$ and $\frac{1}{2}$
- begin to understand that fractions are numbers

Concepts covered next year include

- equivalence between fraction families
- relating fractions to division
- introduction to decimals
- equivalence between fractions and decimals

Assessment points

- positioning fractions on a number line
- recognising simple fractions of shapes and sets
- beginning to recognise equivalence between simple fractions

Chief misconceptions

- misunderstanding the meaning of the numerator and denominator
- thinking that the larger the denominator the larger the fraction
- confusing simple fractions with mixed fractions
- seeing fractions as shapes rather than as numbers

Fractions 1.1 Fractions of shapes

Objectives ● recognise and create the fractions $\frac{1}{2}$, $\frac{1}{3}$, $\frac{1}{4}$, $\frac{1}{5}$, $\frac{1}{10}$ in the context of shapes
 ● know that the denominator shows the number of equal parts into which the whole has been divided
 ● know that e.g. ten tenths make one whole

Key idea	The number at the bottom of a fraction shows how many equal parts the whole has been divided into.

Teaching model

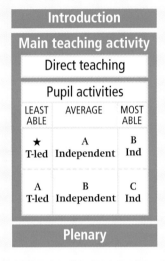

Key words fraction, equal, whole, one half, quarter, third, fifth, tenth

You need

set of place value cards (tens and units) for each pair
paper shapes: round 'pizza', square 'chocolate cake', rectangular 'cherry pie', round 'birthday cake'

Introduction: oral work and mental calculation

about 5 minutes
Use place value cards. Hold up a number to 20. Children, working in pairs, show the number that is half yours. Repeat for doubling.

Main teaching input and pupil activities

Direct teaching

about 15 minutes
1. Write $\frac{1}{2}$ on the board. Ask children to tell you what they know about it (one half, it is what you get when you divide something into two equal pieces). Hold up the 'pizza' and cut it into two equal pieces. *The 2 at the bottom of the fraction tells us how many equal pieces we have to divide the pizza into. The 1 at the top tells us how many of the pieces we want.*
2. Repeat for $\frac{1}{4}$ and the square 'chocolate cake'.
3. Write $\frac{1}{3}$ on the board. *Here is another fraction. How many equal pieces will we cut our cherry pie into?* (3) Draw lines across the 'cherry pie' to show the 3 pieces. We *call these thirds. How many thirds do we want?* (1) Cut 1 piece, $\frac{1}{3}$, from the pie.
4. *We want to share this birthday cake between five children. What fraction of the cake will they each get?* Invite children to come up and write the fraction on the board, discussing how they worked out how to do it. Repeat for tenths.

Pupil activities

about 20 minutes
CORE   Independent   TB page 42 CM 27
A and **B** Children identify fractions.
SUPPORT ★ Teacher-led
Repeat the Direct teaching activities using the
shapes on TB page 42.
EXTENSION C   Independent   TB page 42
Children make up fractions of their own.

Optional adult input to groups

Core: Are children using the correct names for
the fractions?
Extension: Encourage children to be ambitious in
their choice of numbers.

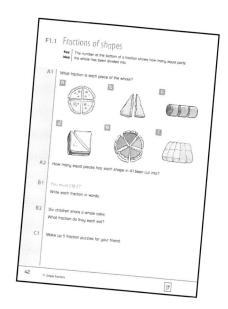

Plenary

about 10 minutes

Key idea	The number at the bottom of a fraction shows how many equal parts the whole has been divided into.

1. Write a fraction on the board. Children hold
   up cards to show how many parts the whole
   has been divided into.
2. *How many equal pieces would I have if I divided one
   whole into tenths?* Repeat for other fractions.
3. Invite children to tell everyone when they use
   fractions in everyday life.

Homework suggestion

Children draw a picture of a food that they cut
into equal pieces for the people they live with
and write the fraction of the whole that each
receives.

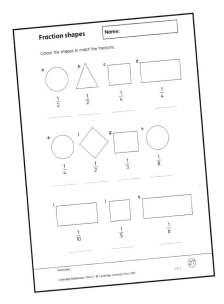

Fractions 1.2 Equal and unequal

Objectives • recognise what is not $\frac{1}{2}$, $\frac{1}{3}$, $\frac{1}{4}$, $\frac{1}{5}$, $\frac{1}{10}$ of whole shapes

Key idea	A part of a shape is only a fraction of the whole if the shape has been divided into equal parts.

Teaching model

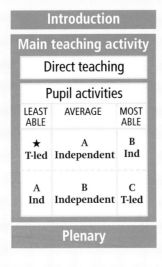

Introduction

Main teaching activity

Direct teaching

Pupil activities

LEAST ABLE	AVERAGE	MOST ABLE
★ T-led	A Independent	B Ind
A Ind	B Independent	C T-led

Plenary

Key words part, equal, not equal, divided, fraction

You need

IP 6   43   CM 28

fraction cards from CM 36

set of place value cards (tens and units) for each pair

hoops labelled: halves, not halves, quarters, not quarters, thirds, not thirds, tenths, not tenths, fifths, not fifths

a copy of CM 28 for each child

interlocking cubes

Introduction: oral work and mental calculation

about 5 minutes

Hold up a fraction card. Children hold up the number that the whole has been divided into.

Main teaching input and pupil activities

Direct teaching

about 20 minutes

1. Ask children which balloons or baskets on IP 6 show halves. Ask them how they know (2 equal parts). Repeat for other fractions.
2. Point to kite number 31. *This kite is divided into 2 parts. Are these halves? Why not?* Ask children to find a kite which is divided into halves (numbers 64 and 71). Repeat for other kites. Invite children to pose the questions.
3. Ask children to draw lines on their kite on CM 28 which divide it up into fractions or not fractions.
4. Children swap kite pictures with their neighbour. Children put the kite in the labelled hoops as appropriate. Discuss the placing of the kites, encouraging children to remind each other why they were placed where they were.

Pupil activities

about 15 minutes

CORE **Independent** TB page 43

A and **B** Children identify fractions and not fractions.

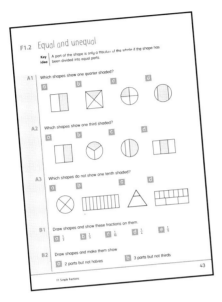

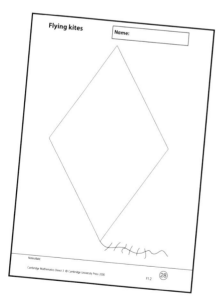

SUPPORT ★ **Teacher-led**

Fold a piece of paper in 2 so that 1 part is larger than the other. *Are these halves?* Ask a child to cut along the fold line and then compare the 2 pieces. Repeat for folds that do make halves, and for quarters and not quarters.

EXTENSION C Teacher-led

Children make shapes with interlocking cubes in different colours, to show fractions and 'not fractions', to test the rest of the class in the plenary.

Optional adult input to groups

Core: Children should look at the number of parts as well as whether they are of equal size.

Plenary

about 10 minutes

Key idea	A part of a shape is only a fraction of the whole if the shape has been divided into equal parts.

1. Ask children to explain their textbook work.
2. Children who did the support activity can show the pieces that they made by cutting and why these were fractions or 'not fractions'.
3. Invite members of the extension group to pose their puzzles.

Homework suggestion

Draw 2 kites which are divided up into the same number of parts: one into equal parts, the other not.

Fractions 1.3 Fractions of a set

Objectives
- divide sets into equal subsets
- identify $\frac{1}{2}$, $\frac{1}{3}$, $\frac{1}{4}$, $\frac{1}{5}$, $\frac{1}{10}$ of sets of objects to 20
- identify a fraction shown
- find half of all numbers to 30

Key idea | **We can find fractions of sets.**

Teaching model

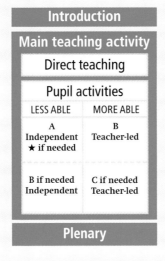

Introduction	
Main teaching activity	
Direct teaching	
Pupil activities	
LESS ABLE	MORE ABLE
A Independent ★ if needed	B Teacher-led
B if needed Independent	C if needed Teacher-led
Plenary	

Key words   part, equal, divided, fraction

You need

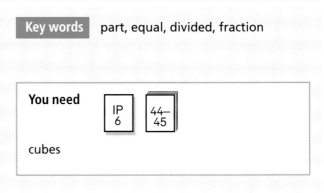

IP 6   44–45

cubes

Introduction: oral work and mental calculation

about 5 minutes

Count on and back in steps of 2, 5 and 10 from 0 to 30.

Main teaching input and pupil activities

Direct teaching

about 15 minutes

1. Put out 12 cubes. Ask 3 children to come to the front. *I'm going to give them each a third of these cubes. How many will Sita get? How can we work this out? We want to make 3 equal groups.* Demonstrate sharing the cubes between the three subsets. *How many did Sita get? Have the others each got the same? So one third of 12 is 4.*

2. Repeat for 20 cubes and 5 children, making one fifth each.

3. *Who will find one tenth of 20? One twentieth of 20?*

4. Use IP 6. Point out the people who are watching the flying machines. *How many people are there?* (30)

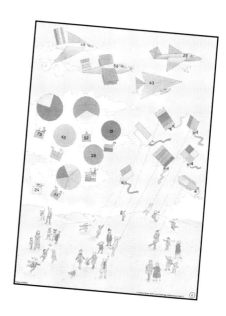

Ask someone to find $\frac{1}{2}$ of them by making 2 equal groups.
Repeat for $\frac{1}{3}$, $\frac{1}{5}$ and $\frac{1}{10}$.
Show how to use cubes to help.

Pupil activities

about 20 minutes

LESS ABLE   Independent   TB page 44

CORE A

Children find fractions of subsets.

SUPPORT ★

Children find fractions of sets of small numbers.

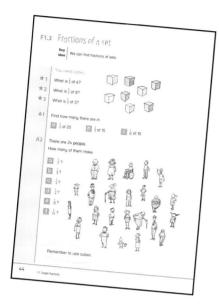

MORE ABLE   Teacher-led   TB page 45

CORE B

Children identify a fraction of a set that is shown and also find halves of numbers to 30.

EXTENSION C

Children make up their own fractions of sets using the information on IP 6.

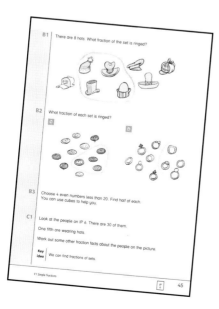

Optional adult input to groups

Less able: check that children are making the correct number of subsets.

Plenary

about 10 minutes

Key idea	We can find fractions of sets.

1. Ask children to explain their strategies for finding fractions of sets.
2. What are the halves of numbers to 30? Can anyone see a pattern in the answers?
3. Invite the class to ask the extension group questions about the work that they did.

Homework suggestion

Learn 5 halves of numbers to 30.

Fractions 1.4 Further fractions of a set

Objectives
- solve problems involving fractions
- find half of an odd number of objects

Key idea	We can find half of an odd number.

Teaching model

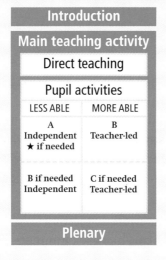

Key words part, whole, fraction, divided between/among

You need

paper 'cake' shapes, cubes, number cards 0–30, small paper shapes for children to cut in half

Introduction: oral work and mental calculation

about 5 minutes

Hold up a number card. Children put up one hand if it is odd and both hands if it is even. Count on and back in steps of 2 from 0 or 1 to 40.

Main teaching input and pupil activities

Direct teaching

about 15 minutes

1. Put out 1 'cake'. *How much cake does each child get when 1 cake is divided equally between 2 children?* ($\frac{1}{2}$) Write this on the board. Repeat for 2 cakes (1 each).

2. Put out 3 'cakes'. *How much does each child get when 3 cakes are divided equally between 2 children? Let's share them out.* Give each child 1 cake and ask children to say what should be done with the one left over so that each child gets the same amount. *So each child gets one and a half cakes.* Write this on the board. Show children how the number is split into the whole number part and the fraction part. Say it together.

3. Repeat for up to 6 cakes. *Can anyone see a pattern?* (Half of an odd number has a whole number and a half in the answer; half of an odd number is the half of the preceding even number plus half.)

Pupil activities

about 20 minutes

LESS ABLE   Independent   TB page 46
CORE A
Children find half of all numbers up to 30.
SUPPORT ★
Children use paper shapes and cut them where necessary to help them find half of numbers to 30.

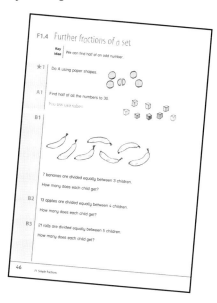

MORE ABLE   Teacher-led
CORE B   TB page 46
Children find fractions of other numbers that do not result in whole number answers.
EXTENSION C   TB page 47
Children halve numbers repeatedly, looking for patterns in their answers.

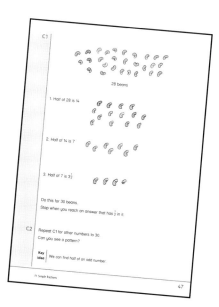

Optional adult input to groups

Less able: Check whether children have recognised that half of an odd number will not be a whole number.

Plenary

about 10 minutes

Key idea	We can find half of an odd number.

1. Say the halves of numbers to 30 round the class. Discuss the patterns in the answers.
2. Ask children who did activity B to talk about their work.
3. Invite the class to ask the extension group about their work on repeated halving.

Homework suggestion
Look at the first digit of a telephone number you know. What is half of that number? Repeat for the other digits.

Fractions 1.5 Simple fraction problems

Objectives
- consolidate recognition of $\frac{1}{2}$, $\frac{1}{3}$, $\frac{1}{4}$, $\frac{1}{5}$, $\frac{1}{10}$ of shapes and sets of objects
- solve simple word problems involving factions

Key idea	We can solve problems involving fractions.

Teaching model

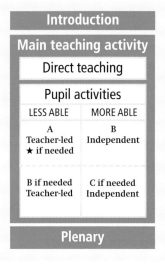

Key words part, fraction, one whole, half, third, quarter, fifth, tenth

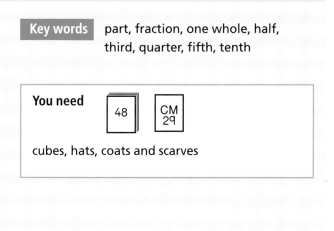

You need 48 CM 29

cubes, hats, coats and scarves

Introduction: oral work and mental calculation

about 5 minutes

Practise halving and doubling numbers to 20.
Count on and back in steps of 3 and 4 from 0 to 50.

Main teaching input and pupil activities

Direct teaching

about 15 minutes

1. Ask a child to choose a colour, e.g. blue. Make a tower 15 cubes high that is $\frac{1}{5}$ blue and the rest a mix of other colours. *Who can tell me what fraction of my tower is blue?*

2. Ask for a volunteer to come up and make a tower 16 cubes high that is $\frac{1}{4}$ red. Other children can give advice on how they can go about this.

3. Ask 8 children to stand up. *Give half of them a pencil to hold. How many would that be? Give one quarter of them a ruler to hold. How many would that be?*

4. Ask 12 children to stand up.
   Give 3 of them hats to wear,
       6 of them coats to wear,
       4 of them scarves to wear.
   Ask what fraction of the children are wearing each garment.

Pupil activities

about 20 minutes

LESS ABLE Teacher-led CM 29
CORE A
Children follow the instructions to find different fractions of a group of 12 people.

SUPPORT ★
Children use cubes to help them calculate the fractions.

MORE ABLE Independent TB page 48
CORE B
Children make towers and structures from cubes which meet different criteria.

EXTENSION C
Children answer more word problems involving fractions.

Optional adult input to groups
More able: Ask children to say what number of cubes they need to satisfy the criteria.

Plenary

about 10 minutes

Key idea	We can solve problems involving fractions.

1. Invite children to talk about their pictures. How did they work out how many people to give boots, scarves, ... to?
2. Ask children who made cube structures to explain what they did and why. If children have produced shapes where all the coloured cubes are together ask: *What if the yellow cubes were spaced out along the tower, would $\frac{1}{4}$ of the tower still be yellow?*
3. Ask the extension group to explain their strategies.

Homework suggestion
Children make up a fraction puzzle like the one on CM 29.

Fractions 2.1 Thirds

Objective ● recognise $\frac{2}{3}$ of shapes and sets

Key idea	We can find two thirds of shapes and sets.

Teaching model

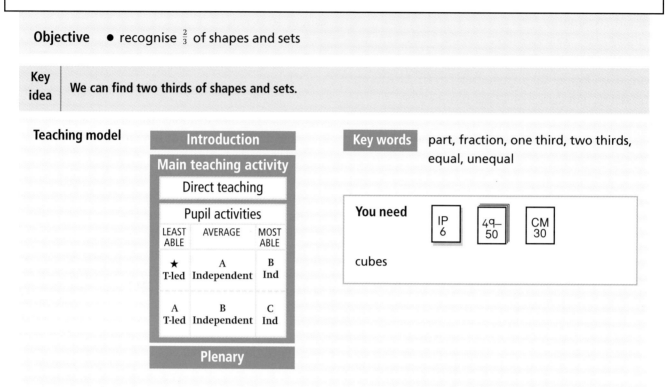

Key words part, fraction, one third, two thirds, equal, unequal

You need	IP 6	49–50	CM 30
cubes			

Introduction: oral work and mental calculation

about 5 minutes

Count on and back in steps of 3 from 0 to 30.

Main teaching input and pupil activities

Direct teaching

about 15 minutes

1. Indicate balloon 52 on IP 6. *How many equal parts has it been divided into? What fraction of the balloon is yellow?* Write $\frac{1}{3}$ on the board. *How many thirds are blue?* Show children how to write $\frac{2}{3}$.

2. Draw a rectangle on the board. Ask a volunteer to divide it up into thirds. Ask someone to write two thirds in words next to the rectangle. Ask someone else to colour in two thirds.

3. Repeat with a square.

4. Put out 6 cubes. Ask someone to divide the set into thirds. *If we have one third of the cubes in the set, how many will we have?* (2) *If we have two thirds of the cubes in this set, how many will we have?* (4)

5. Repeat for 9, 12 and 15 cubes.

Pupil activities

about 20 minutes

CORE   Independent TB page 49 CM 30
A and B Children identify $\frac{1}{3}$ and $\frac{2}{3}$ of shapes and sets.

SUPPORT ★ Teacher-led   TB page 49
Remind children that thirds are of equal size. Work through A with them.

EXTENSION C Independent   TB page 50
Children answer word problems about the picture in the textbook.

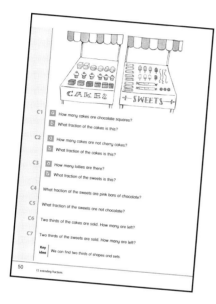

Optional adult input to groups

Core: Help children to use their knowledge of what $\frac{1}{3}$ is to find out what $\frac{2}{3}$ is.
Extension: Check that children are reading the 'not' questions carefully.

Plenary

about 10 minutes

Key idea	We can find two thirds of shapes and sets.

1. Ask children to explain how they know that some of the shapes were not divided into thirds.
2. Discuss the copymaster pictures.
3. *What other questions could be asked about the picture on page 49 of the textbook?*

Homework suggestion
Draw a picture with 12 things in it. Make up 3 'thirds' questions to ask about it.

Fractions 2.2 Halves and quarters

Objectives
- recognise $\frac{2}{3}$, $\frac{3}{4}$
- recognise equivalence between $\frac{1}{2}$ and $\frac{2}{4}$

Key idea	Two quarters make one half.

Teaching model

Introduction

Main teaching activity

Direct teaching

Pupil activities

LEAST ABLE	AVERAGE	MOST ABLE
★ Ind	A Independent	B T-led
A Ind	B Independent	C T-led

Plenary

Key words part, fraction, same as, two/three quarters

You need

IP 6 | 51–52 | CM 31

washable spirit pen, cubes

Introduction: oral work and mental calculation

about 5 minutes

Count on and back in steps of 4 from 0 to 40.

Main teaching input and pupil activities

Direct teaching

about 15 minutes

1. Point to balloon 73 on IP 6. *How many equal parts has it been divided into?*
   What fraction of this balloon is shaded red? ($\frac{1}{4}$).
   What fraction is not shaded red? Yes, $\frac{3}{4}$.

2. *How did you know the fractions the balloon was divided into? Yes, there were four equal parts, so the balloon was divided into quarters.*

3. Draw a circle on the board. *Can anyone shade $\frac{3}{4}$ of this circle?*

4. Repeat with rectangle, square.

5. Look at balloon 24. *Can anyone shade $\frac{1}{2}$ of this circle? Draw a line across the circle to divide it into quarters. What have I divided the circle into now? How many quarters fit into half the circle? $\frac{2}{4}$ is the same amount as $\frac{1}{2}$.*

6. Count out 2 groups of 8 cubes and give them to 2 children. Put a barrier between them so that they can't see what the other is doing, but the rest of the class can see both children. Ask one child to find $\frac{1}{4}$ of their cubes. *Now, find 2 quarters. Don't say how many you've got.* Ask the other child to find half of their cubes. Compare the two amounts. *Are they the same or different?*

Pupil activities

about 20 minutes

CORE   Independent   TB pages 51 and 52

A and B   Children identify halves and quarters.

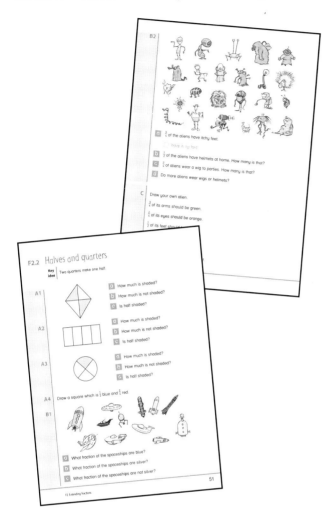

SUPPORT ★ Independent   CM 31

Children compare $\frac{1}{2}$ and $\frac{2}{4}$.

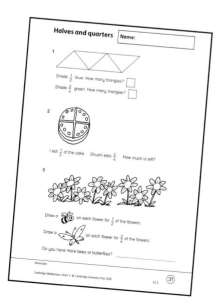

EXTENSION C   Teacher-led   TB page 52

Children draw their own aliens. Encourage them to choose numbers other than 4 for the arms and legs.

Optional adult input to groups

Core: Check that children understand that $\frac{2}{4}$ and $\frac{1}{2}$ are equivalent.

Plenary

about 10 minutes

Key idea	Two quarters make one half.

1. Extension children can show their aliens. Invite the rest of the class to ask them questions.
2. Ask children who did the support activity to talk about their work and to ask the core group questions about theirs.
3. *Would you rather have $\frac{1}{4}$ of a cake, or $\frac{2}{4}$? ... Why? ... What would you rather have: $\frac{2}{4}$ of a cake, or $\frac{1}{2}$? ... Why? ... What would you rather have: $\frac{1}{4}$ of a bag of sweets, or $\frac{2}{4}$? ... Why? ... What would you rather have: $\frac{2}{4}$ of a bag of sweets, or $\frac{1}{2}$? ... Why? ... Ask the children to make up similar questions.*

Homework suggestion

Ask children to find an empty food packet (or draw their own) which contains something they can make up $\frac{1}{2}$ and $\frac{2}{4}$ questions about.

Fractions 2.3 Tenths

Objectives
- introduce shapes where several tenths are shaded
- recognise fractions that are several parts of a whole
- recognise the equivalence of $\frac{5}{10}$ and $\frac{1}{2}$

Key idea	Five tenths make one half.

Teaching model

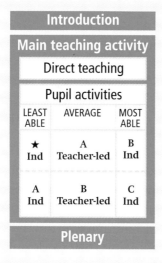

Key words part, fraction, same as, tenths, one whole

You need

cut-up copies of CM 32 so each child will have a strip

cubes, dice marked $\frac{1}{2}$, $\frac{2}{10}$, 0, $\frac{1}{10}$, $\frac{1}{10}$, $\frac{1}{10}$

Introduction: oral work and mental calculation

about 5 minutes

Count on and back in steps of 10 from 0 to 100.

Practise doubling and halving numbers to aid agility when looking for equivalence.

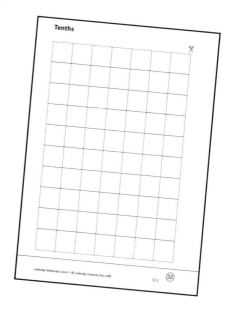

Main teaching input and pupil activities

Direct teaching

about 15 minutes

1. Give each child a strip from CM 32. *What fractions do these sections show?* Count the sections together. *Yes, there are 10. So what do we call these fractions? ... Yes, tenths.*
2. Write $\frac{1}{10}$ on the board. *We know there are 10 tenths in one whole, so how many tenths are there in each half? ... Fold your strip in half to find out... Yes, there are 5.*
3. *Why must there be the same number of tenths in each half?* (Because halves are the same size.)
4. Ask a child to come up and colour in 3 tenths of your strip. *Is this more or less than one half?*
5. Repeat for other numbers of tenths.

Pupil activities

about 20 minutes

CORE   Teacher-led   TB pages 53 and 54

A and **B** Children identify tenths and halves.

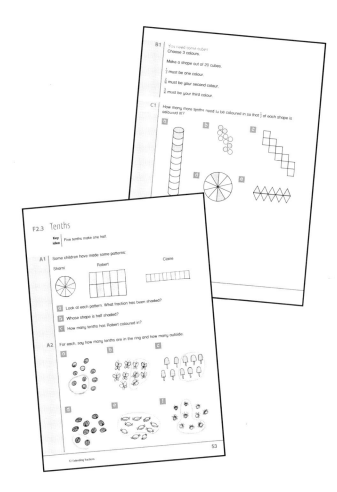

EXTENSION C   Independent   TB page 54

Children work out how many more tenths are needed to make one half.

Optional adult input to groups

Support: Check that children understand that $\frac{5}{10}$ and $\frac{1}{2}$ are equivalent.

Plenary

about 10 minutes

Key idea	Five tenths make one half.

1. Support children explain their game to the rest of the class.
2. Children show their cube models.
3. Extension children explain their activity. What did they find difficult?
4. Ask childen to show you different numbers of tenths by holding up their tenths strips folded back to reveal the right number of spaces.

Homework suggestion

Play 'Fill my pie' with someone at home. They can make 6 fraction cards instead of using a dice.

SUPPORT ★ Independent   CM 33

Children play 'Fill my pie'. Each pair needs a copy of the sheet and a dice.

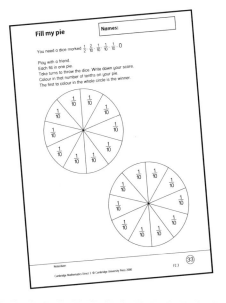

Fractions 2.4 Fractions of shapes

Objectives
- create simple unit and non-unit fractions in the context of shapes
- know that $\frac{3}{10} + \frac{7}{10} = 1$, for example

Key idea	If we know what fraction of the whole we have, we can work out what the whole shape looks like.

Teaching model

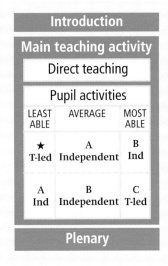

Key words   one whole, part, equal, same as

You need   IP 6   55   CM 34   CM 35   CM 36

Blu-Tack, round paper 'cake' portions showing fractions: $\frac{1}{2}$, $\frac{3}{4}$

Introduction: oral work and mental calculation

about 5 minutes

Revise number bond work to facilitate speed. For example $\frac{7}{10} + \frac{3}{10} = 1$ requires knowledge of the maths fact that $7 + 3 = 10$.

Main teaching input and pupil activities

Direct teaching

about 15 minutes

1. Stick the half cake portion on the board. *This cake was round. Someone has taken a piece without asking. How much is left? How much has been taken? How do you know?* Guide children to talk about their knowing that there are two halves in one whole and that if you've only got one then you are missing one because $1 + 1 = 2$. Ask a child to come up and draw the missing portion of cake to check the prediction.

2. Repeat for the three quarter portion.

3. Look at balloon 45 on IP 6. *How many equal parts is the basket divided into? So what fraction is each part?* ($\frac{1}{6}$) *What fraction is purple?* ($\frac{4}{6}$) Write this

in words on the IP. *What fraction is orange?* ($\frac{2}{6}$) Write this on the IP. *All the purple sixths and all the orange sixths go together to make one whole basket so we can write $\frac{4}{6}$ and $\frac{2}{6}$ make 1 whole.*

4. Repeat for other baskets, balloons and the tails on the flying machines on the IP.

Pupil activities

about 20 minutes

CORE   Independent

A TB page 55

Children work out what fraction is needed to complete the whole.

B CM 35

Children find different ways of making fraction sentences.

SUPPORT ★ Teacher-led   CM 34

Children colour in fractions to make fraction sentences.

EXTENSION C   Teacher-led   CM 36 (cut up for them)

In pairs children play 'Make one whole':

They spread out the fraction cards face down, and take turns to turn over 2 cards; if the cards make one whole they win the cards. The player with the most cards at the end wins.

Optional adult input to groups

Core: Encourage children to use their knowledge of number facts rather than counting the fractions on the page.

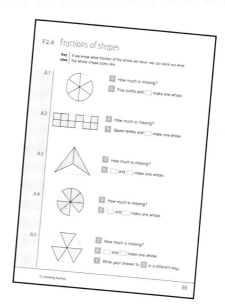

Plenary

about 10 minutes

Key idea	If we know what fraction of the whole we have, we can work out what the whole shape looks like.

1. Ask children to talk about the patterns they made for the tails of the flying machines. How many different ways did they find? How did knowing the number facts of 6 help?

2. Divide the class into 2 teams and play 'Make one whole'. Remind children to use the number facts they know to help them.

3. Show children a fraction card and ask them to tell you how much more you need to make one whole.

Homework suggestion

Children play 'Make one whole' at home.

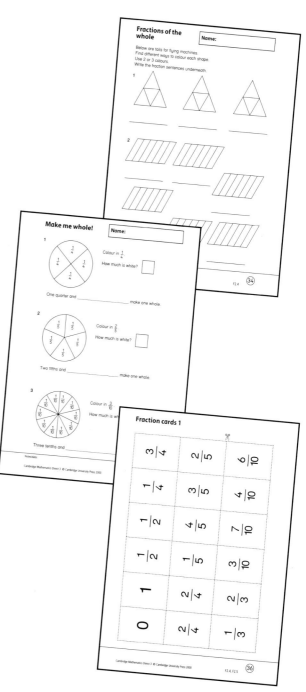

Fractions 2.5   More fractions of sets

Objectives
- find non-unit fractions of sets of objects
- recognise equivalent fractions of sets of objects

Key idea	We can find $\frac{3}{4}$, $\frac{2}{5}$, $\frac{4}{10}$, ... of sets of objects.

Teaching model

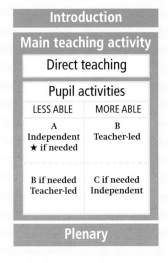

Key words   one whole, part, equal, same as

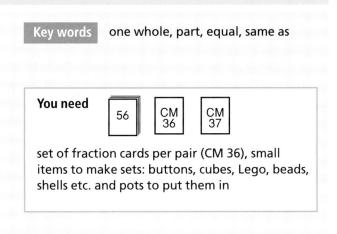

You need | 56 | CM 36 | CM 37 |

set of fraction cards per pair (CM 36), small items to make sets: buttons, cubes, Lego, beads, shells etc. and pots to put them in

Introduction: oral work and mental calculation

about 5 minutes

Hold up a fraction card and ask children working in pairs to hold up how much more is needed to make one whole.

Main teaching input and pupil activities

Direct teaching

about 15 minutes

1. Put out 12 shells. *I want to give Craig* $\frac{1}{4}$. *How many is that? How many would I have left? What fraction is that? How did you work that out?* Discuss methods of working.

2. Put out 15 buttons. *I want to give Sarah* $\frac{1}{3}$. *How many is that? How many would I have left? What fraction is that?*

3. *I have 10 beads. I give Shari* $\frac{3}{5}$. *How many do I give her?*

4. Repeat for other numbers and fractions.

5. *I have 16 sweets. I want to give Robert 8 of them. Should I give him half or two quarters?* (They're the same.)

6. Repeat for other equivalent fractions.

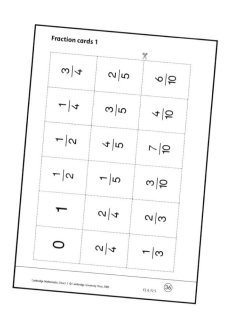

Fraction cards 1

$\frac{3}{4}$	$\frac{2}{5}$	$\frac{6}{10}$
$\frac{1}{4}$	$\frac{3}{5}$	$\frac{4}{10}$
$\frac{1}{2}$	$\frac{4}{5}$	$\frac{7}{10}$
$\frac{1}{2}$	$\frac{1}{5}$	$\frac{3}{10}$
1	$\frac{2}{4}$	$\frac{2}{3}$
0	$\frac{2}{4}$	$\frac{1}{3}$

Cambridge Mathematics Direct 3 © Cambridge University Press 2000   F2.4, F2.5   36

Pupil activities

about 20 minutes

LESS ABLE

CORE A   Independent   CM 37

Children find non-unit fractions of sets of objects. Make sure that when they get to the half and whole boxes they look back at the $\frac{2}{4}$ and $\frac{4}{4}$ boxes.

CORE B   Teacher-led   TB page 56

Children investigate other sets.

SUPPORT ★ Independent   CM 37

In pairs children do the core activity by splitting up the total number of cubes into pots, e.g. when dividing 12 into quarters they share 12 cubes out between four pots. They combine the contents of the pots to find two quarters, three quarters, ...

MORE ABLE

CORE B   Teacher-led   TB page 56

Children investigate other sets.

EXTENSION C   Independent   TB page 56

Children investigate equivalent fractions.

Optional adult input to groups

Extension: Help children to see equivalent fractions for 30 objects.

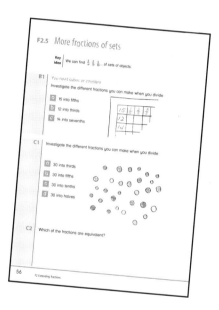

Plenary

about 10 minutes

| Key idea | We can find $\frac{3}{4}$, $\frac{2}{5}$, $\frac{4}{10}$ ... of sets of objects. |

1. Ask the different groups of children to talk about what they did and found out.
2. Play 'Make one whole' as a class again. Remind children to use the number facts they know to help them.
3. *How many tenths do I need to make one half?* Repeat for other simple equivalences.

Homework suggestion

Children look for empty packets and packaging with fractions on them for a class collection.

Fractions 3.1 0–1 number line

Objectives
- compare and order $\frac{1}{4}$, $\frac{1}{2}$, $\frac{3}{4}$
- position $\frac{1}{4}$, $\frac{1}{2}$, $\frac{3}{4}$ on a unit number line
- know that $\frac{1}{4}$ is half of $\frac{1}{2}$

Key idea | We can find $\frac{1}{4}$ by halving and then halving again.

Teaching model

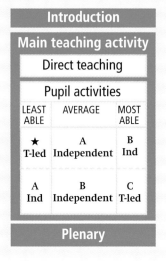

Introduction
Main teaching activity
Direct teaching
Pupil activities

LEAST ABLE	AVERAGE	MOST ABLE
★ T-led	A Independent	B Ind
A Ind	B Independent	C T-led

Plenary

Key words part, fraction, one whole, one half, one quarter, three quarters, equal

You need IP 7   57   CM 38

set of place value cards and strip of paper per child

paper shapes such as circles, squares, rectangles that can be cut in half and half again

scissors, glue, small objects, e.g. cubes, beads, shells, buttons

Introduction: oral work and mental calculation

about 5 minutes

Call out tens numbers to 100. Children show half with place value cards.

Call out a number 0–20. *I'm thinking of a number. This is half of that number. Show me the number I'm thinking of.*

Main teaching input and pupil activities

Direct teaching

about 15 minutes

1. Ask children in pairs to tell each other about what they already know about fractions (part of a whole, notation). Ensure that children are clear about what 'one whole' means. Write the words on the board.

2. Give each child a strip of paper. *Write 0 at one end and 1 at the other.* Ask them to fold it in half. *Open up your paper. What do we notice about each half?* (identical, equal) *How many halves in a whole?* Ask a volunteer to write 'half' and '$\frac{1}{2}$' on the board. Children write $\frac{1}{2}$ on the fold line.

3. Ask children to fold their strip of paper in half again. *Now let's fold our half in half. Open up your paper. How many equally sized parts have we got now?* (4) *So what fraction is each part?* ($\frac{1}{4}$) Ask a child to write 'quarter' and '$\frac{1}{4}$' on the board. Children write $\frac{1}{4}$, $\frac{1}{2}$, $\frac{3}{4}$ and $\frac{4}{4}$ on the fold lines and at the end of the strip.

4. *Who can explain what we have just done?* (made a half and then found quarters by making a half of the half) *It is useful to know that quarter is half of half as this makes an easy way to find a quarter.*

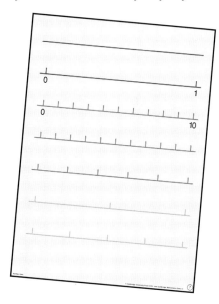

5. *If I draw a line along my strip of paper like this, I can make a number line from 0 to 1 with fractions on it.* Copy the marks onto the 0–1 number line on IP 7. Count along it and back together, reminding children that $\frac{2}{4}$ is the same as $\frac{1}{2}$.

6. *Looking at the number line, tell me a number that is less than $\frac{1}{2}$ | $\frac{3}{4}$ ... bigger than $\frac{1}{4}$.*

7. Put out a simple collections, e.g. 12 cubes. Show children how to find a quarter by halving the set and then halving again: *We halve the set of cubes. That gives us 6 in each half. Now we halve one of the halves and that gives us 3. How could we check whether this is one quarter of 12?* (try making 4 groups which each have 3 in them)

8. Ask children to find one quarter of 16 by halving and halving again. Model informal recording on the board, e.g. 16 – Half is 8 – Half is 4 – So quarter of 16 = 4

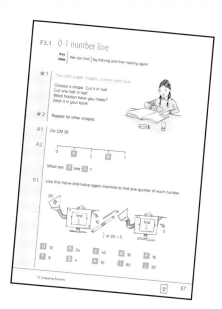

Pupil activities

about 20 minutes
CORE
A Independent TB page 57 and CM 38
Children find quarters of shapes by halving and halving again.
B Independent TB page 57
Children find quarters of numbers by halving and halving again.
SUPPORT ★ Teacher-led TB page 57
Children find quarter of paper shapes by cutting them in half and then in half again.
EXTENSION C Teacher-led
Ask children to use the halve-and-halve-again strategy to find $\frac{1}{4}$ of large numbers in everyday life, such as objects in the classroom, e.g. sheets of paper, books, pencils, and ask them to record their work clearly in their own way.

Optional adult input to groups
A and B: Check that children understand what they are doing by asking them to explain what is happening.

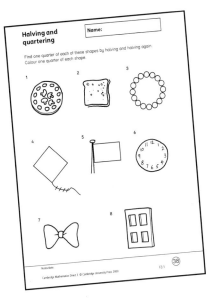

Plenary

about 10 minutes

Key idea	We can find $\frac{1}{4}$ of a shape or set by halving and then halving again.

1. Ask the support group to show their shapes to the rest of the class and explain what they did.
2. Ask children to tell you what they have learnt this lesson. Some ideas will be specific, e.g. 'I know that a quarter of 16 is 4', some general, e.g. 'I know how to find a quarter of a number.' Make a list on the board.

Homework suggestion
Children create a pattern on squared paper using whole, half and quarter squares.

Fractions 3.2 Number line to 10 (quarters)

Objectives
- mark quarters, halves, and three quarters on a number line to 10
- count on and back in steps of $\frac{1}{4}$, $\frac{1}{2}$
- compare and order mixed fractions involving $\frac{1}{4}$, $\frac{1}{2}$, $\frac{3}{4}$

Key idea	Fractions are numbers. We can position them on a number line.

Teaching model

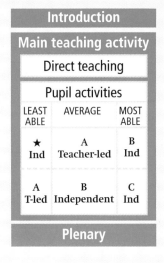

Key words part, fraction, one whole, half way

You need

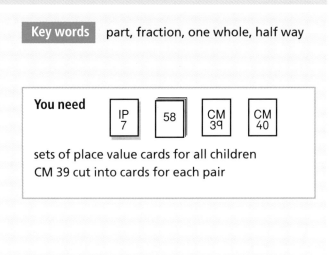

sets of place value cards for all children
CM 39 cut into cards for each pair

Introduction: oral work and mental calculation

about 5 minutes

1. Count to 40 and back in 2s from different starting points.
2. Count to 40 and back in 4s from different starting points. (Have numbers marked on a counting stick if necessary.)

Main teaching input and pupil activities

Direct teaching

about 20 minutes

1. Look at IP 7. *Let's say the whole numbers from 0 to 10 along the 0–10 number line.*
2. *What is the number half way between 0 and 1? Draw the half-way mark and write '$\frac{1}{2}$' on the line.*
3. *What is the number half way between 1 and 2? Draw the half-way mark and write '$1\frac{1}{2}$' on the line.*
4. Repeat for the other numbers to 10 and ask for volunteers to mark the half numbers with a coloured pen. (Look at the markings on the line and adjust with children until reasonably accurate.)
5. *Let's count along the line now: 0, $\frac{1}{2}$, 1, $1\frac{1}{2}$, 2, …*
6. *What is the number half way between zero and one half? Draw the half-way mark and write '$\frac{1}{4}$' on the line.*
7. *What number is half way between one half and one? Draw the half-way mark and write '$\frac{3}{4}$' on the line.*
8. Repeat for the other quarters to 10 and ask for volunteers to mark the quarter numbers with a different colour pen.
9. Practise counting along and back from different starting points in steps of halves, then quarters.

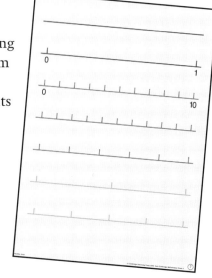

10. Ask volunteers to come out and write mixed numbers, e.g. $2\frac{1}{2}$, on the board.
    All look at the notation, and correct together if necessary.
    Identify the difference between the digit 2 in the whole number and the half number.
    Locate $2\frac{1}{2}$ on the number line.
    Practise with several mixed numbers to ensure children understand the notation.

11. Look at three mixed numbers on the board, e.g. $1\frac{1}{2}$, $2\frac{1}{4}$, $\frac{3}{4}$.
    What do we notice about these numbers? (There is no whole number in $\frac{3}{4}$, there are 2 numbers containing quarters.)
    Order the numbers, smallest to largest, with the children suggesting and explaining the sequence. Locate the numbers on the number line to check the order.

Pupil activities

about 15 minutes
CORE

A Teacher-led CM 39
Children work in pairs with a set of cards from CM 39.
Spread out the cards face down in front of you. Take turns to pick up 3 cards and place them in order, smallest to largest, then record for your partner to check.
Replace the cards and shuffle them around after each turn.
Vary the game: Pick 5 numbers each time. Order largest to smallest. One child picks a central number and the other finds a smaller and a larger number...

B Independent TB page 58
Children find mixed fractions on number lines.

SUPPORT ★ Independent CM 40
This gives practice at placing half and quarter numbers on sections of a number line to 10.

EXTENSION C Independent TB page 58
Children write their own questions about their chosen segment of number line.

Optional adult input to groups
Support: Check that children understand why the half numbers are marked in red and blue.
Extension: Help children to focus on what might be between the numbers.

Plenary

about 10 minutes

Key idea	Fractions are numbers. We can position them on a number line.

1. Extension group ask their questions.
2. Play 'Fraction bingo': In pairs, children draw a 3×3 grid and write 9 numbers between 0 and 4 in the cells (a mixture of fractions and whole numbers). Call out clues to fractions for children to work out, e.g. a number between $2\frac{1}{2}$ and $3\frac{1}{2}$. Record each clue.
   First challenge: Get 3 numbers in a row – check answers together.
   Second challenge: Complete the whole grid.

Homework suggestion
Design a simple card game involving fractions that uses CM 39, for example:
'Pairs': Spread out the cards face down. Take turns to pick up 2 cards. If they are both whole or half numbers etc. keep the cards. Practise playing your game at home and prepare to share it with rest of class.

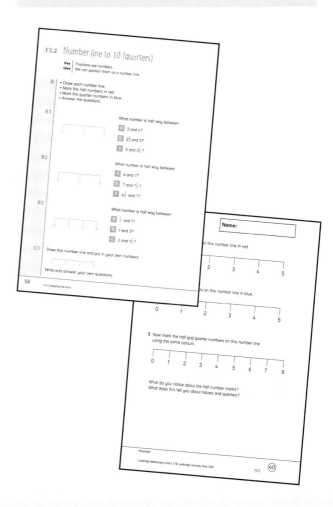

Fractions 3.3 Tenths on a number line

Objectives
- mark tenths on a unit number line
- compare and order fractions involving tenths and halves

Key idea | Knowing that $\frac{5}{10} = \frac{1}{2}$ helps us to compare tenths and one half.

Teaching model

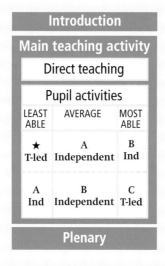

Key words — part, fraction, one whole , half way, tenths

You need

IP 7 | 59–60 | CM 41

sets of digit cards for all children

Introduction: oral work and mental calculation

about 5 minutes

Count to 100 and back in 10s.

Play 'Make 10': Call out a number; children show the number to make it up to 10. Call out 2 numbers; children show the number needed to make their total up to 10.

Main teaching input and pupil activities

Direct teaching

about 20 minutes

1. *In this lesson we are going to learn about tenths and compare tenths and halves.*
2. *Tell me a number between 2 and 3. What number is half way between 9 and 10?*
3. Write $\frac{1}{10}$ on the board and ask children to tell you about it. (It is a tenth, one part of a whole one split into 10 equal parts.)
4. Count in tenths from 0 to one whole and back to 0.

5. Look at the 0–1 number line on IP 7. Draw in the half-way mark. *What number is here? How many tenths is that?* Ask a volunteer to mark $\frac{5}{10}$ in a coloured pen.
6. Ask volunteer(s) to mark the other tenths numbers with a different coloured pen.
7. Practise counting on and back along the number line from different starting points.
8. Ask children to say whether $\frac{3}{10}$ is greater or smaller than $\frac{1}{2}$.

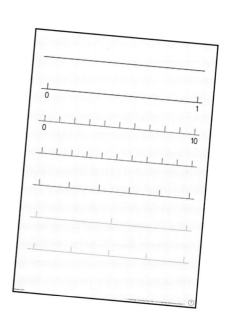

Pupil activities

about 15 minutes

CORE   Independent   TB page 59

A In pairs children play a game comparing tenths and halves.

B Children find the missing numbers on a number line.

SUPPORT ★ Teacher-led   CM 41

Children compare tenths with one half.

EXTENSION C   Teacher-led   TB page 60

Children look at tenths between other whole numbers.

Optional adult input to groups

Core: Check that children are comparing their numbers with 5 tenths.

Support: Help children to find the $\frac{5}{10}$ division and compare the coloured part with it.

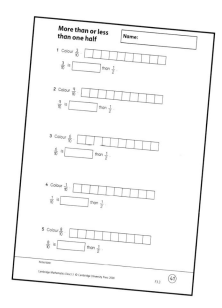

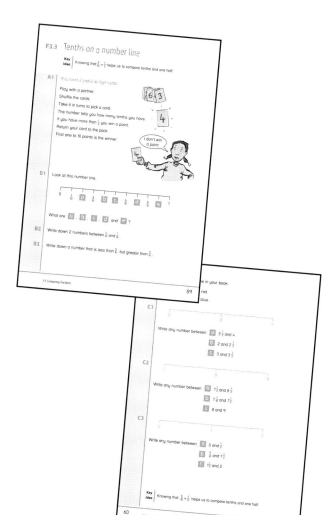

Plenary

about 10 minutes

Key idea	Knowing that $\frac{5}{10} = \frac{1}{2}$ helps us to compare tenths and one half.

1. Support group talk about the strips and which numbers are bigger than one half.
2. Play 'Fraction bingo': In pairs, children draw a 2×2 grid and write 4 numbers between 0 and 1 in the cells. Call out clues to fractions for children to work out. Keep a record of your clues for checking the winning card.

Homework suggestion

Design a flag(s) with a pattern made of tenths where half is one colour.

Fractions 3.4 Estimating fractions

Objectives
- recognise that for a given shape or quantity $\frac{1}{2}$ is greater than $\frac{1}{4}$
- make estimates of fractions of shapes or quantities

Key idea	We can use our knowledge of fractions to estimate fractions of shapes and quantities.

Teaching model

Introduction
Main teaching activity
Direct teaching
Pupil activities

LEAST ABLE	AVERAGE	MOST ABLE
★ T-led	A Independent	B Ind
A T-led	B Independent	C Ind

Plenary

Key words fraction, one whole, half way, half, quarter, tenth

You need

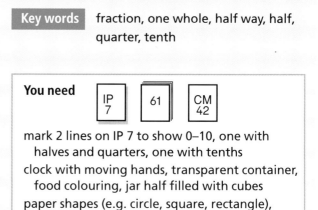

mark 2 lines on IP 7 to show 0–10, one with halves and quarters, one with tenths

clock with moving hands, transparent container, food colouring, jar half filled with cubes

paper shapes (e.g. circle, square, rectangle), paper, glue, scissors

Introduction: oral work and mental calculation

about 5 minutes

Display the number line showing halves and quarters. Practise counting along and back in steps of a half and then a quarter.

Display the tenths number line. Call a number, e.g. $4\frac{2}{10}$, and ask children to call back the number before or the number after.

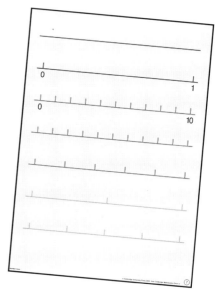

Main teaching input and pupil activities

Direct teaching

about 15 minutes

1. Look at practical examples of halves and quarters, e.g. folded paper, collections of objects (8 pencils, 4 children etc.), and establish that $\frac{1}{2}$ is always greater than $\frac{1}{4}$.
2. Look at a clock face. Identify $\frac{1}{4}$, $\frac{1}{2}$, $\frac{3}{4}$ way round the clock face. Move the hands of the clock into these positions or close to these positions and ask children to tell the time (quarter past 3, about half past 6, etc.).

3. Fill a transparent container with coloured water (made with a few drops of food colouring). Show children the whole then tip some away. Ask children to estimate the fraction of water left. Encourage estimation in tenths as well as halves and quarters.

   Pour more water away and repeat, drawing out language of fractions and estimation, and asking children to justify their estimates.
4. Hold up the jar of cubes. *This jar holds about 100 cubes when it is full. About how many are left?*

Pupil activities

about 25 minutes

CORE

A Independent   CM 42

Children practise estimating fractions.

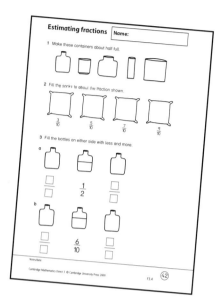

B Independent   TB page 61

Children use their knowledge of fractions to estimate times and quantities.

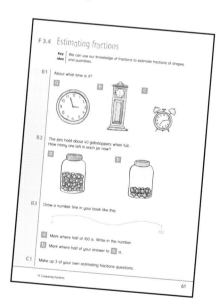

SUPPORT ★ Teacher-led

Fold paper shapes into halves and quarters, label $\frac{1}{2}$ and $\frac{1}{4}$ of each shape and stick them into books to reinforce the concept of $\frac{1}{2}$ being larger than $\frac{1}{4}$. Repeat the Direct teaching activities.

EXTENSION C   Independent   TB page 61

Children make up their own estimating questions.

Optional adult input to groups

Core: Encourage children to work out what $\frac{1}{2}$ would be, and then look for the required fraction in relation to that.

Plenary

about 10 minutes

Key idea	We can use our knowledge of fractions to estimate fractions of shapes and quantities.

1. Ask the support group to show their folded paper work as a reminder that a half is greater than a quarter.
2. Ask the core group to show their work and to describe how they carried it out. Encourage other groups to ask questions, and the core group to answer using the correct language.
3. The extension group ask their questions and add their own observations.

Homework suggestion

Practise at home filling a container with water, tipping some away and drawing and estimating the fraction left. Children record what they do.

Fractions 3.5 Fraction patterns

Objectives
- revision of block with emphasis on language and notation including that of equivalence and ordering
- investigate a general statement about familiar fractions
- recognise simple patterns and relationships, generalise and predict

Key idea	Finding patterns in fractions helps us to solve problems.

Teaching model

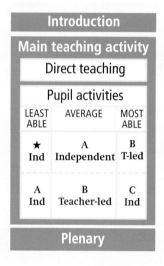

Introduction
Main teaching activity
Direct teaching
Pupil activities

LEAST ABLE	AVERAGE	MOST ABLE
★ Ind	A Independent	B T-led
A Ind	B Teacher-led	C Ind

Plenary

Key words part, fraction, one whole, half, quarter, tenth

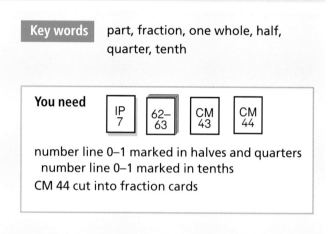

You need IP 7 62–63 CM 43 CM 44

number line 0–1 marked in halves and quarters
number line 0–1 marked in tenths
CM 44 cut into fraction cards

Introduction: oral work and mental calculation

about 5 minutes

1. Show children fraction cards, e.g. $\frac{9}{10}$. Ask a child to say the fraction shown.
2. Say a fraction, e.g. three quarters, and ask children to write and show it.
3. Play 'Make one whole':
   Call out a fraction, e.g. $\frac{6}{10}$, and ask children to write and show the fraction needed to make it up to one whole ($\frac{4}{10}$). N.B. use IP 7 to display number lines marked in halves and quarters to help children who need support.

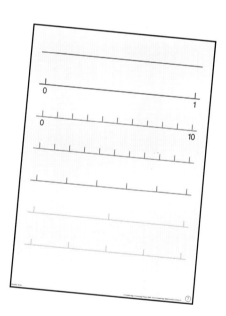

Main teaching input and pupil activities

Direct teaching

about 15 minutes

1. *In this lesson we are going to use what we know about fractions to look for patterns and relationships.*

2. Draw 3 cakes on the board and divide one in half, one in quarters and one into tenths.
3. Ask for volunteers to come out and shade in half of each cake.
   Write $\frac{1}{2} = \frac{2}{4} = \frac{5}{10}$
4. Add another cake. *Can anyone shade half in another way? How many halves are there? How many whole cakes are there?* Count together: $\frac{1}{2}, 1, 1\frac{1}{2}, 2$

Pupil activities

about 25 minutes

CORE

A Independent   TB pages 62–63

Children complete a selection of puzzles and patterns involving tenths and thirds.

B Teacher-led   TB page 63

Children investigate general statements about fractions.

Can anyone explain how to change halves to wholes?
(Divide by 2.)

Is it the same rule for changing odd numbers of halves to mixed numbers? (Yes)

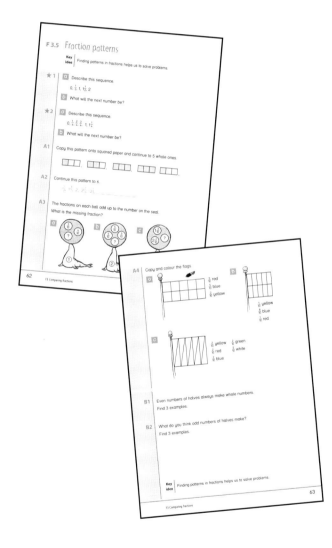

SUPPORT ★ Independent   TB page 62

Children describe fraction sequences.

EXTENSION C   Independent   CM 43

Children support general statements with their own examples and then write a general statement of their own.

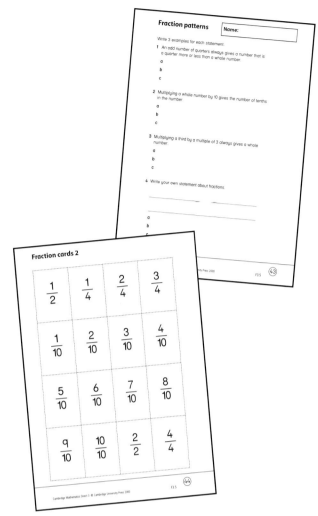

Optional adult input to groups

Support: Encourage children to look for the rule for each sequence.

Extension: Help with recording.

Plenary

about 10 minutes

Key idea	Looking for patterns in fractions helps us to solve problems.

1. Ask the support group to talk about their sequences.
2. Discuss the general statements from B.
3. Invite the class to ask the extension group questions.

Homework suggestion

Ask children to make their own quiz of 10 questions about fractions with the answers.